Acclaim for WILLIE MORRIS's

My Dog Skip

"This book is both a loving tribute to his companion and a lyrical remembrance of vanished innocence."   —*People*

"A memoir of [Morris's] beloved boyhood friend, companion and fellow prankster. . . . It's a rich experience all around."
                    —*The New York Times Book Review*

"This marvelous memoir, like the Oscar-winning *Forrest Gump*, takes you back to an era of innocence."   —*Los Angeles Times*

"If the rat race is getting to you, if you long for long hazy summer days of wandering barefoot around town seeking whatever adventure could arise, if you had a dog that was THE dog . . . *My Dog Skip* is for you . . . Skip lives on in a million fond memories."
                    —*Times Record News* (Wichita Falls, Texas)

"Morris's clean, spare, emotionally laden prose captures his youth and America at mid-century with crystal clarity and draws the reader into reading and rereading beautifully turned sentences and phrases. . . . This is a book that begs to be read aloud. No one who had a dog as a child can remain unaffected by this gem of a book."   —*Flint Journal* (Michigan)

"This is the kind of book that makes readers smile."
                    —*Patriot Ledger*

BOOKS BY WILLIE MORRIS

My Dog Skip

North Toward Home

Yazoo

The Last of the Southern Girls

James Jones: A Friendship

The Courting of Marcus Dupree

Terrains of the Heart

Always Stand in Against the Curve

Homecomings (with William Dunlap)

Faulkner's Mississippi (with William Eggleston)

After All, It's Only a Game (with Lynn Green Root)

New York Days

Good Old Boy (a juvenile)

Prayer for the Opening of the Little League Season
(with Barry Moser)

WILLIE MORRIS

My Dog Skip

Willie Morris is the author of *North Toward Home,*
New York Days, and two novels. As the imaginative
and creative editor of *Harper's,* he was a major influ-
ence in changing our postwar literary and journalistic
history.

My Dog Skip

WILLIE MORRIS

Vintage Books

A DIVISION OF RANDOM HOUSE, INC.

NEW YORK

The Library of Congress has cataloged the Random House
edition as follows:
Morris, Willie.
My dog Skip / by Willie Morris. — 1st ed.
p.   cm.
ISBN 0-679-44144-1
1. Morris, Willie—Childhood and youth.   2. Authors, American—
20th century—Biography.   3. Pet owners—Mississippi—Biography.
4. City and town life—Mississippi.   5. Boys—Mississippi.
6. Dogs—Mississippi.   I. Title.
PS3563.08745Z473   1994
813'.54—dc20   94-41637
[B]
Vintage ISBN: 0-679-76722-3

BOOK DESIGN BY CATHRYN S. AISON

Manufactured in the United States of America
3579B864

To Anne-Clinton and Winston Groom,
to their dog Forrest Gump—
and to everyone else who ever loved a dog

CONTENTS

CONTENTS

My Dog Skip

————•••••••————

A Faded Photograph

I CAME ACROSS a photograph of him not long ago, his black face with the long snout sniffing at something in the air, his tail straight and pointing, his eyes flashing in some momentary excitement. Looking at a faded photograph taken more than forty years before, even as a grown man, I would admit I still missed him.

It was 1943. I was nine years old and in the third grade when I saw him for the very first time. I had known we were getting him. My father had ordered him from a dog breeder he had heard about in Springfield, Missouri. Daddy had picked him up at the Illinois Central train depot, and when I came home that day from school he had just put the wire portable kennel on our back porch. I opened the door to the box and looked inside. I saw a little puppy drinking water from a container attached to the bottom. He glanced up at me.

"Come here, boy," I said.

He walked on unsteady legs toward me. I was sitting on the floor of the porch when he came out. He jumped into my lap and began nuzzling my hand with his nose. When I leaned toward him, he gave me a moist lick on my chin. Then he hugged me.

I led him into the house and gave him some puppy food in a dish. Then I followed him as he gingerly explored every room in the house. That night he jumped into my bed and stared at me, as if he were looking me over. Then, perhaps because he missed his mother in Missouri, he went to sleep in my arms. I was an only child, and he now was an only dog.

This was the first of our many days and years together. We named him Skipper for the lively way he walked, but he was always just Skip to me.

We had had a whole string of dogs before. When I was a very little boy we had big bird dogs, and then two purebred English smooth-haired fox terriers like this one, and I got to know all about dogs, a most precocious expert—their funny or crazy moods, how they looked when they were hungry or sick, when they were ready to bite and when their growling meant nothing, what they might be trying to say when they moaned and made strange human noises deep in their throats.

None of those other dogs ever came up to this one. You could talk to him as well as you could to many human beings, and *much* better than you could to some. He would sit down and look you straight in the eye, a long, mesmerizing gaze, and when he understood what you were saying he would turn his head sideways, back and forth, oscillating his whole body like the pendulum on a clock. Before going to sleep at night, with him sitting next to my face on the bed as he always did in such hours, I would say, "First thing tomorrow I want you to get your leash and then come get me up, because we're gonna get in the car and go out to the woods and get some *squirrels*," and the next morning sure enough he would get his leash, wake up both my father and me, walk nervously around the house with the leash in his mouth while we ate breakfast, and then lead us out to the car. Or I could say, "How about a little *swim?*" and his face would light up and he would push open the back door with his paws and escort me the quarter of a mile down the back alleyway to the swimming hole under the cypress near the bayou. Or, "Bubba's comin' over here today, and we're gonna play some *football*," and he would listen closely to this, and go out and wait around in front of the house and pick up Bubba's scent a block down the street and come tell me he was on his way. Or, "Skip, how about some *catch?*" and he would get up and walk into the front room, open a door in the antique cabinet with his improbable nose, and bring me his tennis ball.

I watched him grow up from the puppy who came to us from Missouri to the sleek, dexterous, affectionate creature who could do all these things, and more. He knew my father by the name of Big Boss. My mother was Bossie, and I was Little Boss or, interchangeably, Willie. (I called *him*, depending on the mood, Skip, Old Skip, and Boy. I have learned that when you love somebody, you will address him or her by different names.) Sometimes my father would hide in a closet and I would ask, "Skip, where's Big Boss?" and he would search the whole house, looking on every bed and under every chair and table until he arrived at the right closet, and began scratching it with his paws.

The town where Old Skip and I grew up together was an unhurried and isolated place then. About ten thousand people lived there, of all races and origins, and it sat there crazily, half on steep hills and half on the flat Delta. Some of the streets were not paved, and the main street, stretching its several blocks from the Dixie Theater down to the bend in the river, was narrow and plain, but down along the quiet, shady streets, with their magnolia and pecan and elm and locust trees, were the stately old houses that had been built long before the Civil War, slightly dark and decaying until the descendants became prosperous enough to have them "restored," which usually meant one coat of white enamel.

All this was before the big supermarkets and shopping centers and affluent subdivisions with no sidewalks and the monster highways and the innocence lost. It was even before there was television, and people would not close their doors and shut their curtains to watch the quiz games or the comedy hours or the talk shows where everybody talks at once. We would sit out on our front porches in the hot, serene nights and say hello to everyone who walked by. If the fire truck came past, we all got in our cars to follow it, and Skip was always the first to want to go. The houses were set out in a line under the soft green trees, their leaves rustling gently with the breeze. From the river sometimes came the melancholy echo of a boat's horn.

I knew the place then better than I did my own heart— every bend in every road, every house and every field, the exact spot where the robin went for her first crocus. It was not in my soul then, only in my pores, as familiar to me as rain or grass or sunlight. The town was poor one year and rich the next; everything in it pertained to cotton, and hence to usury and mortgage, debenture and labor. We lived and died by nature and followed the whims of the timeless clouds. Our people played seven-card stud against God.

It was a sly and silent town then, and Skip and my friends and I absorbed its every rhythm and heartbeat and the slightest sounds from far away. I loved those funny silences. The whole town was also abundant with alleys behind the paved thoroughfares inherited from an earlier day, little vagrant pathways running with scant design or reason behind the houses and stores and barns and chicken yards and gardens. You could get away with anything in those alleys. How Skip adored the freedom of them!

It was a lazy town, all stretched out on its hills and its flat streets, and over the years Skip also grew to know almost every house, tree, street, and alley. Occasionally he wandered around the town by himself, and everybody of any consequence knew who he was. Unbelievable as this may seem, Skip had the most curious and spooky way of sensing—don't ask me how—where I might be at any given moment, what a later day called ESP.

Our neighborhood was on one of the broad thoroughfares. In our side yard was a row of immense pecan trees shaped at the top like witches' caps, and in the back a huge field, vined and bosky. On the front lawn was a full, towering oak, one of Skip's favorite trees in the entire town.

Every time I shouted *"Squirrel!"* Skip would charge on the oak tree and try to climb it, sometimes getting as high as five or six feet with his spectacular leaps. This would stop traffic on the street in front of the house. People in cars would see him trying to shinny up the tree and would pull up to the curb and watch. They would signal to other passersby and point toward Skip, and these people would pull over too. They would gaze up into the tree to see what he was looking for, and, after a respectable pause, ask me, "What's he got up there?" and I would say, "Somethin' small and mean." They seldom recognized that Skip was just practicing.

This exercise was nothing to compare with football games, however. I cut the lace on a football and taught Old Skip how to carry it in his mouth, and how to hold it so he could avoid fumbles when he was tackled. I instructed him how to move on a quarterback's signals, to take a snap from center on the first bounce, and to follow me down the field. Ten or twelve of my comrades and I would organize a game of tackle in my front yard. Our side would go into a huddle, Skip included, and we would put our arms around one another's shoulders the way they did in real huddles at Ole Miss or Tennessee, and the dog would stand up on his hind legs and, with me kneeling, drape a leg around *my* shoulder. Then I would say, "Skip, pattern thirty-nine, off on three"; we would break out of the huddle with Skip dropping into the tailback position as I had taught him. Mutton-head or Peewee or Henjie or Bubba or Big Boy or Ralph would be the center, and I would station myself at quarter-back and say, "Ready, set, one . . . two . . . *three*"; then the center would snap the ball on a hop to Skip, who would get it by the lace and follow me downfield, dodging would-be tacklers with no effort at all, weaving behind his blockers, spinning loose when he was cornered, sometimes balancing just inside the sidelines until he made it into the end zone. We would slap him on the back and say, nonchalantly, "Good run, boy," or when we had an audience: "Did you see my block back there?" Occasionally he would get tackled, but he seldom lost his grip on the ball, and he would always get up from the bottom of the pile and head straight for the huddle. He was an ideal safety man when the other side punted, and would get a grip on the second or third hop and gallop the length of the field for a touchdown. After consid-erable practice, I succeeded in teaching him the "Statue of

Liberty" play, always shouting *"Statue of Liberty"* to him and our teammates before the play unfolded. I would take the snap from center and fade back in a low crouch, less a crouch than a forty-five-degree list, holding the ball behind my shoulder as if I were about to pass, all the while making sure the loosened lace was at a convenient angle. Skip, stationed at the left-end position, would circle around behind me, taking the lace of the pigskin between his teeth, then moving with deft assurance toward the right side of the line of scrimmage, where I was leading interference, whereupon he would follow his usual phalanx of blockers to the enemy's end zone for another spectacular score. *"Look at that dog playin' football!"* someone passing by would shout, and before the game was over we would have an incredulous crowd watching from cars or sitting on the sidelines, just as they did when he was after squirrels. The older men especially enjoyed this stunning spectacle. Walking down the sidewalk in front of the house, they would stop and let go with great whoops of astonishment: "Man, that's *some* dog. Can he catch a pass?"

For simple gratification, however, I believe Skip enjoyed our most imaginative intrigue above any other, and there are people still living in the town who will testify to it.

In that place and time, we began driving our parents' cars when we were thirteen years old; this was common practice then, and the town was so small that the policemen knew who you were, and your family, although they of course expected you to be careful. When I started driving our old four-door green DeSoto, I always took Skip on my trips around town. He rode with his snout extended far out the window, and if he caught the scent of one of the boys we knew, he would bark and point toward him, and we would stop and give that person a free ride. Skip would shake hands with our mutual friend, and lick him on the face and sit on the front seat between us. Cruising through the fringes of town, I would spot a group of old men standing around up the road. I would get Skip to prop himself against the steering wheel, his black head peering out of the windshield, while I crouched out of sight under the dashboard. Slowing the car to ten or fifteen, I would guide the steering wheel with my right hand while Skip, with his paws, kept it steady. As we drove by the Blue Front Café, I could hear one of the men shout: *"Look at that ol' dog drivin' a car!"*

Later we would ride out into the countryside, past the cotton fields and pecan groves and winding little creeks on the dark flat land toward some somnolent hamlet consisting of three or four unpainted stores, a minuscule wooden post office with its porch stacked with firewood in the wintertime, and a little graveyard nearby. Here the old men in overalls would be sitting on the gallery of the general store with patent-medicine posters on its sides, whittling wood or dipping snuff or swatting flies. When we slowly came past with Skip behind the steering wheel I heard one of them

yell, *"A dog! A dog drivin'!"* and when I glanced slightly above
the dashboard I sighted him falling out of his chair over the
side of the porch into a privet hedge. One afternoon not
long after that Henjie and Skip and I were out and about in
the same country vicinity when far up the gravel road we
saw a substantial congregation of humanity emerging from
a backwoods church after a revival meeting. A number of
the people, in fact, were still shouting and wailing as they
approached their dusty parked cars and pickup trucks. I
stopped the car and placed Skip at his familiar spot behind
the steering wheel; then we slowly continued up the road.
As we passed the church, in the midst of the avid ca-
cophony a woman exclaimed: *"Is that a dog drivin' that car?"*
The ensuing silence as we progressed on by was most hor-
rendously swift and pervasive, and that sudden bucolic
hush and quell remained unforgettable for me, as if the very
spectacle of Old Skip driving that green DeSoto were
inscrutable, celestial, and preordained.

······· 2 ·······

Mutual Mischief

THERE WAS SOMETHING in the very air of a small town in the Deep South then, something spooked-up and romantic, which did funny things to the imagination of its bright and resourceful boys. It had something to do with long and heavy afternoons with nothing doing, with rich slow evenings when the crickets scratched their legs and the frogs made murmuring music, with plain boredom, perhaps with an inherited tradition of making plots. We had to work our imaginations out on something, and the less austere, the better. To this day I have never doubted that Old Skip understood all this better than any dog in history.

As we grew older, he and I collaborated in other diverse ruses, one of them against a little boy named John Abner. My friends and I told him we would give him a quarter if he would walk alone, carrying a flashlight, at nine o'clock one night, halfway through the spooky town cemetery to the "witch's grave"—the resting-place of the demon who had burned down the town in 1904, which was marked now with a heavy chain, with one link missing where she had escaped. John Abner consented. Two of our conspirators promised to accompany him to the gates at nine and send him alone up the road. At eight-thirty Ellis Alias, nicknamed Strawberry, and Skip and I went to the cemetery. It was a still, moonlit night in early June; the light of the sun was just going out on the horizon, giving the evening an eerie glow before the coming of the dark. Strawberry stationed himself ten yards from the witch's grave in a clump of bushes. He had a long stick, with a white pillowcase attached to the end; I had only my silver trumpet, which I was just then learning to play in the junior band, and I hid behind some trees on the opposite side; Skip crouched there next to me. As we waited for our victim, I noticed a man walking up the road about fifty yards away, taking a shortcut to Brickyard Hill. I signaled to Strawberry to wait and took out my trumpet. Pressing the valves halfway down, I played a long, ghastly, moaning wail, as loud as the horn would go. With that, Skip's ears fluttered and he let loose with a shrill, terrifying howl, as if he were baying at the moon. The man gave a little hop-skip-and-jump, listened again, and then took off at a steady gait up into the woods, while we doubled over and all but rolled on the ground with joy. Then we returned to our posts. I had brought with me a pair of lengthy cotton strings and the cardboard replica of a skeleton I had bought at the nickel-and-dime store. I proceeded to tie this grotesque ghoul to Skip's back.

Soon we heard the faint sound of footsteps on the gravel, and there was John Abner, a frightened little boy walking stealthily through the trees, looking all around and flashing his light in every direction. When he got within a few steps of the witch's grave, Strawberry all of a sudden held the stick out from the bushes and waved the pillowcase. Then I blew a solemn high note on my trumpet, and descended to the same moan I had used on the man taking the shortcut. With that, I pushed Skip out from under the trees. Since he knew the poor victim and recognized him, he rushed impetuously toward him. When we looked out, all we could see was a wisp of dust on the road, and we heard the sound of small feet moving fast, Skip with his skeleton in torrid pursuit.

Old Skip was with us the Halloween night several of us went out to one of Peewee's father's pastures not far from our school building to fetch a cow. We knew our schoolteachers would be rehearsing their faculty play shortly after dark on that evening, and we surreptitiously led the cow down one of the town's alleyways onto the school grounds, then through the back door of the auditorium. We tied the rope from the cow's neck to a seat on the aisle, leaving it a good amount of slack to roam around. As we were accomplishing this, I noticed Skip sitting on his haunches staring inquisitively at the cow, and the cow staring right back at him. Skip glanced at me: What manner of creature is this? he seemed to be saying. I believe he perceived we were involved in something of immense consequence.

We retired to some hedges near the auditorium windows as darkness fell. From the street we saw the football coach emerge from his pickup truck and walk toward the auditorium, entering it through the front door; we knew it was the football coach's responsibility to turn on the lights before the other teachers arrived. We snuck up to one of the windows and looked inside, barely able to make out the silhouette of the coach groping his way down the aisle in the darkness. When he bumped into the cow's horns, he emitted a terrorized shriek of such acoustical dimensions that even Skip began to bark, and we got out of there fast.

When my comrades and I were thirteen years old (and Skip three) we ascertained the house where some of the women held their Wednesday-afternoon prayer meetings. One morning, following the cookbook, we baked two dozen oatmeal cookies in our kitchen, using every ingredient just as the book said, and then for good measure we added a mixture of castor oil, dill pickle juice, and milk of magnesia. "What else?" Henjie asked. I looked down at Skip, who had been following our activities with his usual intense attachment. Then I glanced across to the bottom shelf of the kitchen cabinet and saw his worm medicine for dogs, flea-

and-tick powder, and ear ointment. Using an eggbeater, we put these also into our mixture. When the cookies were cool we gift-wrapped them and pasted on a card that read, "To the ladies from all the people in town." Then we crept through the bushes to Sister Craig's house and placed the gift inside the screen door. Later we peered through the window as Sister Craig served the cookies; I propped Skip's head near the ledge so he could watch too. The first guest who bit into an oatmeal cookie chewed on it for a moment, her jaws working politely but with purpose, then spit with such energy that the crumbs landed at a point six feet away, spraying three other guests with the awful stuff. Skip followed this with interest, and then we all slipped happily away. I never knew a dog who cared so passionately for nonsense, especially when he felt he was part of it.

At night when I lay in bed reading, Old Skip would crawl up to me and look at the book, sometimes touching it with his paw. He always wanted to know what I was doing. "You want to read some *Dickens?*" I might ask. When I turned out the light he would go to sleep curled up in the bend of my legs; when it was cold he would root around and scratch at me to get under the covers. First thing in the morning, after he had gone outside for a solitary run, he would bound back into my bed and try to roust me out with his cold nose. If this did not work, he would lightly bite my toes beneath the blanket.

After we both had a breakfast of raisin bran and milk, he would walk with me toward school. The school building was only six blocks down the boulevard from our house, and along the way Henjie would join us, then Bubba, then Rivers Applewhite. Every morning at the same spot, a few yards or so from Rivers's front porch at the street corner near the bayou, he would stop and sit, watching us from afar as we crossed the bridge to the school grounds; then he would turn around and go home. Every afternoon after school he would be at that precise place waiting for me. We would retrace our journey home again, where I would make us both a mayonnaise-and-ketchup sandwich before we commenced our late-afternoon rituals.

Of these many exercises, one involved my throwing sticks for him. He was the best retriever I ever had. I would throw a stick as far as I could, far across the alley behind our house perhaps, or into the deepest recesses of the neighbors' backyards, and then hide in the shrubs or under the house or in the green DeSoto parked in the driveway. Skip would come tearing around with the stick in his mouth and, not finding me where I had been when I threw the stick, would drop it and look everywhere. If he found me under the house, he would crawl in there and lick my nose, as if to suggest I was not as smart as I thought I was. Or he would jump onto the hood of the car or even go into the house to see if I was there.

This game backfired one day; I am not saying Skip was all perfect, for who wants a perfect dog? Bubba and I threw a stick for him far into Mrs. Graeber's yard and then climbed the elm tree in the back of my house, hiding far up the branches among the leaves. It took him half an hour to find us. We watched with superior smirks and stifled laughter as he dropped the stick and roamed everywhere in his search for us, looking on top of the garage and inside the toolshed and in the gullies abutting the alley, even going onto Mrs. Graeber's back porch and into her wisteria vines in his quest. When he finally located us in the tree he became extremely angry. He refused to let us out of that tree. Every time one of us descended, he snapped at our feet with his long white teeth. We sought to soothe him with assuaging talk—"You're a good old boy, Skip" or "How about some raisin bran?"—but we might just as well have been courting Hitler or Tojo or Mussolini. Since no one was around to come to our rescue, we were trapped up there for over two hours until Skip got tired and dozed asleep, and we missed the biggest Cub Scout baseball game of the season.

I have mentioned his high regard for raisin bran. I have never seen a dog with such a haughty distaste for dog food—dog food of all kinds—which he never once touched after his days as a puppy. Put a can of Red Heart on his platter and he would treat it with the disdain of a potentate from the most sublime of palatinates. His preferences were otherwise highly eclectic and included the mayonnaise-and-ketchup sandwiches we ate after school, fried chicken livers, squirrel dumplings, parched peanuts, potato chips, Moonpies, ham hocks, chicken gizzards, cotton candy, and rice and gravy. His favorite food of all, however, was sliced bologna.

After a time we devised an established procedure with my black friend Bozo, who worked behind the meat counter at Goodloe's Grocery Store down the street. I made a small leather pouch and attached it to Skip's collar. I would say, "Skip, go on down to Bozo and get yourself a pound of bologna." Then I would put a quarter in the leather pouch, and Skip would take off down the sidewalk for the store and bring the package back in his mouth, with Bozo's change in the pouch. Bozo enjoyed entertaining his friends with this exercise. They would be standing around, talking baseball or football or some such, and when Bozo heard Skip scratch on the front screen door, he would open the door with a sweeping deferential flourish and tell his companions, "Here's Old Skip shoppin' for a pound of his favorite *food-stuff*," and with another great gesture would negotiate the transaction.

There was a parallel to this. When Bozo opened the leather pouch and found only a nickel, he knew Skip had been dispatched by my father to get the Jackson newspaper. Bozo would roll up the newspaper with a rubber band and Skip would return home with it in his mouth. One day, however, he came back with the *Memphis* newspaper. Daddy subscribed regularly to the Memphis paper, and he was exceedingly upset. He severely admonished Skip, then ordered him to take the paper back and to return with the right one. Skip appeared a few minutes later with the Memphis paper again. In the pouch, I found a note from Bozo: "It ain't the dog's fault. We run out of Jackson papers." My father felt so guilty he gave Skip four fried chicken livers.

In one of those early summers I entered Skip in the local dog contest, a highly regarded event sponsored by the United Daughters of the Confederacy. About five hundred people were in the audience, and since the prize was to be based on good looks and on the tricks the dogs could perform, I felt certain Skip would win. Fifty-two dogs were to participate in the competition. Skip was the thirty-fifth on the program, and when he was announced, I led him onto the stage of the auditorium. Because he was a well-known presence in town, everyone generously applauded. Then a polite silence fell as I got him to walk around the stage two or three times so the judges could examine his posture and the way he carried himself. Now it was time for the tricks.

"Sit down!" I commanded. But Skip had an ornery look in his eyes and would not sit down. Instead he jumped up and barked. *"Lie down and roll over!"* This time he sat down and shook hands. *"Play dead!"* To this he leapt off the stage, ran up the aisle, turned around, and leapt onto the stage again. The spectators began to laugh, and I was growing more and more embarrassed by the minute. *"Sit down!"* I repeated. He rolled over twice and then stretched out contrarily on his

back with all four feet sticking up in the air. When he finally got up, I reached for the tennis ball in my pocket and said, *"Make a catch!"* I tossed the ball in the air toward him. Ordinarily he could have caught such a mundane throw in his mouth with no effort at all, but he let the ball go right by him, conjuring for me in that unsettling instant my readings about the Chicago Black Sox, who threw the 1919 World Series. I had never seen him so difficult. I led him backstage and told him he had made a fool of me. Only later did I comprehend that he did not care about winning trophies and considered the performance of public tricks beneath his dignity. But when the prizes were announced, he tied for first place with Sheriff Raines's big bulldog, a handsome dog named Buck with an impressive brown-and-white forehead, although he slobbered a lot. Super-Doop, the Hendrixes' black Labrador, finished a few points behind Skip and Buck. The judges said they were not impressed with Skip's discipline, but they gave him the prize because he was such a fine-looking dog. In appropriate time I forgave him his irascibility before the judges, and for many years the blue ribbon with the shiny medal attached to it hung proudly on the wall of my bedroom.

Not long after this, when I turned twelve and joined Troop 72 of the Boy Scouts and began working on merit badges, I discovered that not a single member of the town troop had Dog Care. This was hard to fathom, yet true. Numerous of the local boys had earned such unusual merit badges as Sheep Farming, Pigeon Raising, Poultry Study, Reptile Study, Bird Study, and Pulp and Paper, and the smartest older boy in the troop, named J.C., offspring of our dentist, Doc Shirley, not only had acquired all these but also possessed the most arduous merit badge of all, called Signaling, which embraced Morse code, ship codes, and flags, despite the fact that we lived five hundred miles at the very least from the nearest ocean, but even this most diligent of boys did not have Dog Care. With such a distinctive companion as Old Skip, I determined to set a historical precedent, but I needed to have my certificate of authority approved by a practicing veterinarian. I telephoned the town vet, named Dr. Cornelius Jones, to make an appointment, explaining to him my mission. I asked if I should bring my dog with me, and he said he did not deem that necessary.

His offices were in a dark old stone building on Washington Street covered with lush green ivy, and the smells inside of medicines and antiseptics and animals were pungent but not disagreeable. "Since I've never been asked to do this before," he said, "I'll just ask you some questions about your own dog. What's his name?"

"Skip."

He queried me about age, weight, breed, habitudes, and training, and then asked: "What about fleas?"

"What about 'em, sir?" I replied.

"Does your dog have fleas?"

"He's got plenty, yessir."

"How do you rid him of fleas?"

"Well, I pick 'em off him one by one and throw 'em on top of the heater."

This apparently discouraged the doctor. He started in on another line of questioning.

"Do you consider your dog intelligent?"

"Yessir. He may be the smartest dog who ever lived."

"Really? What can he do?"

I told him he could drive a car with a little help and picked up his own bologna at Goodloe's Grocery. Also that he played football.

Once more he gave me a disbelieving glance. "Do you feed him a good diet?"

"Yessir, I sure do."

"How many times a day do you feed him?"

"Oh, I guess about seven or eight."

"Seven or eight!" the doctor said. "Don't you know you're only supposed to feed a dog once a day?" Then, shaking his head, he signed my certificate, making me the first in the county to get Dog Care.

······· 3 ·······

The Woods, Fishing,
and a Skunk

ONE AUTUMN AFTERNOON my father had Old Skip
out for squirrels at the Delta end of the county. There was
a slight rustling in the underbrush. Skip suddenly froze,
sniffed the air, looked intently around, then with a neat
bounding leap crashed in after the sound.

Almost as suddenly he emerged, the most woebegone
dog in the world. A skunk, his dignity intact, strutted roy-
ally out into the opening and down the trail. Skip had the
foul yellow liquid all over him and smelled so putrid we had
to put handkerchiefs to our noses. Even his eyes looked
sick; I can still smell that malevolent odor, which had the
wretched texture of spoiled molasses and a thousand burnt
wires. We walked back to the clearing and wrapped him in
an old blanket, and took him to our backyard as far away
from the house as we could get, and bathed him, not once

but twice, in tomato juice, the oldest remedy in the town for skunk smells. We did not want to lay our eyes on him for days, and until the odor began to wear off he was the most listless and unenthusiastic creature I ever saw. About four or five days later we were sitting in the front room listening to President Roosevelt on the radio. Skip had not been allowed in the house since the assault of the skunk, but now he opened the screen door with his nose and entered. He still smelled bad; my mother was furious. He knocked down an armchair and ran through my father's legs. When we finally caught him, we gave him another tomato juice bath.

Our first dogs were the big ones—Tony, Sam, Jimbo— and since they were bird dogs, they had a fine and natural inclination to hunt. Yet Skip was the best of all, for he trampled the woods with an inborn sense of possibility and adventure.

The Delta woods, when I was a boy, were a living thing for me, and Skip since his earliest days in them loved their commanding excitement and mystery. There were stretches, in the dank swamp-bottoms, that stayed almost wholly dark, even on the brightest of days. The tall thick trees were covered with vines and creeping plants, and on a gray December afternoon the silence was so cold and impenetrable that as a very small boy I would become frightened, and stay close to my father. He taught me how to note landmarks the deeper we went into the woods: one hickory had a gnarled limb, like a broken arm, or the ash next to it was split in two, probably by lightning. Sometimes he would make his own marks, with powder or empty shotgun shells, and he always kept an eye close to his compass. Three or four times in my memory, men had gotten hopelessly lost in these hidden places, and someone would have to organize search parties, or get the sheriff and his deputies to circle round and round in the woods looking for footprints or empty shells or the sign of fires. As we walked along the thin trail, fighting the mosquitoes that swarmed at us despite the ointment we slathered on our skin, the sun would suddenly open up some half-clearing, and giant spiderwebs would shimmer and toss in the light. Daddy would stand dead in his tracks, gesturing to me to be absolutely still, and he would point to a deer farther down the path, looking at us a brief instant before scampering away into the trees. We never hunted deer; my father was against it, and mainly we came to the woods to shoot the wild squirrels, gray and red and sometimes black. The squirrel dumplings my mother would make, in her new pressure cooker, even if we had to spit out the buckshot while eating them, were always worth the hardest day's walk. We had squirrel cookouts in our backyard and invited all my friends. One night Henjie ate four fried squirrels by himself, and Skip could eat two with the blink of an eye and invariably ask for more.

Many was the time we would rise before dawn, and Skip would be waiting for us at the car, such was his agitation to get started toward the woods. We would drive out the flat roads past the dead cotton stalks in the fields, making it to the woods just as the sun was beginning to show. Then we would catch the chatter and rustling of all the birds and beasts, and when we got out of the car Skip would be ready to tear a muscle to get in and see what was there, and once in there would almost immediately start pointing squirrels. In the bottoms the ground was so soggy that our boots would make faint oozing sounds, and our footmarks would slowly fill up with water as we walked; Skip's pawprints would make the same funny sounds, and until he got used to them he would sometimes scratch at them to see if there might be something sinister underneath. And there were days when the air would be so thick with mosquitoes in that raw wilderness, setting upon us in vast and palpable waves, that we had to try to find someplace else or give up and go home. I envied Skip his furry coat when the mosquitoes were troublesome, for to him mosquitoes were neither here nor there, and we would have to beg him to depart with us, such was his affinity for those woods.

These woods were so much a part of our lives, my father's and Skip's and mine, only a half hour's drive or so from town, that I grew up taking them for granted. Only later did I realize that they were the last and largest of the great Delta forests, that it was only at the bottom of that lower triangle of the Delta, where we were, that the remnants of the primordial wilderness had been left untouched by the incursions of man. It was to this spectral country, but closer to the Mississippi River, as I would read many years later in "Delta Autumn," that William Faulkner's character Uncle Ike McCaslin came on his last hunt, having to drive "two hundred miles from Jefferson when once it had been thirty." Little wonder that as I grew older I always in my memory associated these woods with boyhood and Old Skip.

My father and I were in one of these places on December 7, 1941, when I was seven, sometime before I got Skip; I can remember the day by the news that greeted us when we went home. And we had been there many times before then. At first I used a .22, though Daddy once let me shoot his 12-gauge, out of nothing but maliciousness, because after I squeezed the trigger that gun knocked me for a twisting nosedive into the mud. On my twelfth birthday I got a shiny new 16-gauge smelling richly of oil, and the next time we went into the woods I wasted a whole box of shells out of sheer exuberance, and Skip thought I had gone insane.

One afternoon we were walking through a stretch of swamp-bottom with Owen McGinty, one of the town firemen. All of a sudden Owen shouted "Jump!" just as my foot hit something soft and wet, and I jumped with all the enthusiasm I could muster. "Look at *that*," Owen said, rolling out the "*that*," and my father went "*Wheew.*" There was a rattlesnake that must have been eight feet long, right in my path. Even Skip, intrepid in all things, but young at the time, was intimidated by the sight of this menacing serpent, and he backed off a few feet and merely stared at it. "Let the boy shoot him," Owen said, and I aimed my new shotgun and killed him through the head. Owen pulled out his knife and cut off his rattlers and handed them to me. The next day I took the rattlers to school, and my classmates gathered around and said, "He was a *big* 'un." But Miss Abbott, my teacher, found out about it and made me take my trophy home. If the dust from the insides got in your eyes, she said, you would be blinded for life. My father said Miss Abbott got that from an *old wives' tale*.

Several times in the woods around Panther Creek we ran across a man my father knew—a hanger-on, he called him. The man lived right in the middle of the woods, in a little crooked shanty he had made for himself. He had a scraggly black beard and wore beat-up khakis and a slouch hat; in back of his shack was a vegetable garden. The game wardens ignored him, and he lived off the animals he could kill, and made money now and then guiding the deer hunters. My father later told me that the man would eat anything just so it wasn't alive, and even then he might eat it if the gravy was good. Skip took to this man right away, perhaps because the old fellow gave him fried squirrel and allowed him to tease his numerous squawking chickens. "I'll give you five dollars for that dog," he said to me one day. I refused, replying that although Skip had a lot of the woods in him, he was mainly a town dog.

Later, when I lived in England, I saw places that the English called woods, but compared with the Delta swamp-bottoms of that boyhood time they could have been grown in the shop of a florist. Similarly, the lakes where my father, Skip, and I went to fish, compared with the man-made lakes I would see later in Central Texas, were real lakes, of a piece with the stark heavy earth that enveloped them. Their waters were murky and oppressive, and the worst death I ever heard about took place at one of them, when a water-skier got tangled in a school of water moccasins.

We did cane-pole fishing, both to save money and because it was lazier, for we seldom exerted ourselves on these trips to Wolf Lake or Blue Lake or Five-Mile. The most work came the night before, when we hired a couple of children at a quarter an hour and went back to the town dump to catch the roaches for our bait. Directly across the dirt road was a black juke joint, and the sorrowful sounds of blues music wafted across the way as we proceeded on our arcane odyssey. We had a big wire basket with a lid on top, and we would spot the roaches with our flashlights, trap them in our gloves, and drop them into the basket. Need it be said, though this may shock some modern-day hygiene-conscious readers, that Skip was also an agile retriever of roaches? And likewise that he enjoyed going to the dump for its pungent smells and strange discarded paraphernalia and debris?

The next morning, very early, we would drive out into the same Delta country, only not so far, rent a boat from a sharecropper, and spend the day drifting around the water. The fishing itself bored Old Skip, in marked contrast with his exuberant hunting in the forests. My father would sit at one end of the boat, I at the other, with Skip in the middle, and after a decent while he would stretch out on his back with his paws extended upward and doze in the indolent sunshine. I guess he really just wanted to be with us. In the quiet intervals I would ask him, "Want to take a *swim*, Skip?" and he would rouse himself from his slumbers, shake himself three or four times to get the kinks out, and jump overboard, paddling around with only his nose and the top part of his head above the water, and when he had had enough he would swim back to the boat and I would bend down and lift him in.

When the biting was good we might bring home twenty or thirty white perch or bream or goggle-eye; when it was slow we would follow Skip's example and go to sleep in the boat. Whenever we caught a small fish my father would say, "Throw him back. Only the country folks take the little 'uns, and they eat 'em bones and all." We would stop at some crossroads store on the way back to town to stretch and have a Nehi Strawberry or an Orange Crush, and talk about the fishing with the old men who sat out front whittling and chewing Brown Mule, spitting between the cracks of the porch floor and talking all the while. I would get Skip a bag of potato chips, and the three of us—a man, a boy, and a dog—would idly sit on the porch and absorb the lilting prattle of the old men and gaze out at the black people picking cotton in the fields beyond. When we got home my father and I would clean the fish on the back steps and eat them fried, with a crust as delicious as the fish itself. Skip himself might have some fried goggle-eye, but you would have to take the bones out for him first.

I remember one of these afternoons—one of the last, because by that time I was sixteen (which meant Skip had just turned six) and had just about lost interest, and then my father and Skip would go out alone. But on this spring day the weather had taken turns between sunshine and a light rain, and we caught more fish than we had ever caught before. I barely had time to get the line into the water before I could feel the pulling and tugging, and out would come a fish big enough for a feast. The gars were jumping and making splashes all over the lake, and the turtles were diving off their logs, and the fish kept biting away; clearly something was going on under there. On a day such as this Skip would not be permitted his swim, but I could tell he too knew that something auspicious was going on. Then the wind rose and the rain came down in heavy drops, and we paddled to land as quickly as we could and made it to a deserted tenant shack just in time. The drops made little clouds in the dust until the dust itself was wet and muddy, and the rain blew in gusts and rattled hard on the rusty tin roof. We waited there for a long time, until the rain suddenly stopped. Then the sun came out again, and the whole world was wet and cool: the trees heavy and glistening in the sun, and the rich Delta land humming and making its grand noises, the soft fluttering of the leaves, the cries of the birds, the rush of the water. Why do I remember so well the sight of Old Skip in that moment long ago, sitting on his haunches at the edge of the doorway, gazing out, transfixed by the Lord's good earth? Then Daddy said, "We better be gettin' back. If there're any fish left, we'll let 'em alone to grow."

4

War Days

In the first two and a half years of his life, Skip was a war dog, because I was a war boy. He was as much a part of World War II for me as Roosevelt, Churchill, Hitler, and Hirohito.

The war itself was a glorious and incomparable thing, a great panorama intended purely for the gratification of one's childhood imagination, and since Old Skip had an adventuresome heart, I believe he too sensed something momentous was touching our lives. My pals and I never missed a war film; Skip always waited patiently outside the theater until the movie was over and we joined him again. How my contemporaries and I hated the Japanese soldiers, who pried off fingernails, sawed off eyelashes with razors, and bayoneted babies! We loathed the Germans also, but slightly less so, because they looked like us. And the English (with whom we shared "a common tongue") and the Free French and Russians, they were good fellows, and the Chinese were mysterious but friendly, and the Italians (pronounced "*Eye*-talians") were cowardly, but in captivity lovable, full of song, and more than willing to change sides. I promised myself that if the town was ever captured, I would retire to the deepest recesses around Peak Tenereffe with Skip and the other boys as a guerrilla fighter, and if I was ever caught and put before a firing squad, I would yell, *"Long Live America!"*

We climbed Brickyard Hill and stood at its highest pinnacle with prewar Woolworth binoculars searching for any sign of Junkers or Zeroes, whose shapes we had memorized from twenty-five-cent books on enemy aircraft, and when Skip saw us looking up into the heavens *he* looked too, whether mimicking us or not, I was never quite sure. I kept a diary of all the crucial battles, which I followed every day in the pages of the *Memphis Commercial Appeal* and the *Jackson Daily News,* and I kept entries of more personal matters also. I came across this diary not long ago, all shriveled and yellowing, in the same box where I had found Old Skip's photograph. My handwriting on the first page said: "In the event of an emergency contact my dog Skip." One of the entries in my boyish scrawl declared: "Skip is smart. Skip is *very* smart," and went on to describe how only the week before he had supported us in trying to uncover a German spy network in town.

The circumstances were these, the little diary reminded me: Because of the Southland Oil Refinery a few miles from town, and the active flow of commerce on the river, I had surmised that our town had been chosen by Berlin as a prime target, and hence we considered it our responsibility to keep our eyes keenly out for alien espionage agents. On that ominous forenoon the previous week, we had noticed a large blanket hanging on a clothesline behind a house near the town dump with a swastika emblazoned on the cloth! Immediately suspicious, I told my diary, Peewee, Mutton-head, Henjie, Skip, and I hid in a nearby grove of chinaberry trees and for long moments surveyed the house. Three or four enigmatic people kept going in and out. We forthwith hastened to police headquarters and reported our discovery to Sheriff Raines, who was drinking iced tea in a wicker chair on the sidewalk. "Oh, hell," he said. "I know them people," and proceeded to tell us the swastika was an Indian symbol on an old Indian blanket. "That don't matter," he advised us. "You boys and the dog continue to keep your eyes out at all times."

Skip never cared much for the radio, but whenever we listened to Hitler giving a speech on our shortwave at home he had a most uncommon reaction. Cocking an ear to the Führer's burning words and shouts, he would sit there for a moment imbibing this bombast, then with his ears twitch-ing as in pain, begin strutting about the room emitting deranged little howls, his snout lifted mightily upward, much as he had done in the cemetery when we accosted the man making the shortcut. Often was the time we had to turn off the radio to get him to stop. Why did he never once do this when listening to Mussolini? Was this part of his ESP in reading my own moods about matters? Whatever it was, I never knew a dog so down on Hitler.

The boy who had lived in the big white house next door had enlisted in the army when he was seventeen. Now he was fighting in Europe and we exchanged Victory mail, which we called V-mail, and I sent him reports of ballgames and sometimes oatmeal cookies (the good kind). One fabulous day a substantial package came to me from France, and I brought it into my room to open it. Always curious about novel and unexpected items, Skip began poking it with his nose. When I tore off the paper and opened the top of the box, he put his head inside to see what was there. It was a real German helmet, with the name of the soldier—*Willy*—carved inside it, and also a German belt with its engraving, GOTT MIT UNS, and an iron cross, and German money, and postcards of German storm troopers. Skip was intrigued by the helmet; when I placed it on the floor he sniffed it some more, then pushed it around with a paw. Tolbert, an old man who was doing some handiwork around the house, was fascinated with that helmet too. Sometimes I would let him wear it home, and he would walk off down the back alley, doing a goose step the way the Germans did, Skip following with sharp interest right behind him; then he would turn and wave at me, snapping his heels and giving me the "Heil Hitler" sign. Later I wore the helmet, the iron cross, and the belt down Main Street one Saturday afternoon, Skip at my heels. All the country boys standing on the corner came to look them over.

"Gott mit uns," one of them said. "Now what's that supposed to say?"

"God with us," I replied.

"Yeah? Now ain't that somethin'? Them Germans think they got God on *their* side."

In addition to exploring the vicinity for spies, we pursued other constructive patriotic activities, and Skip was closely involved in these lofty schemes also. Dominating this good old time was the image of Franklin D. Roosevelt, our president—his voice on the radio, his face with the dark rings under his eyes on the newsreels. Because of him my father and I planted a big Victory garden in our backyard, raising food on our own because much of it was scarce and we had to have special ration stamps to buy it. We grew long rows of snap beans, tomatoes, beets, radishes, corn, squash, and rutabagas, and a unique breed of swamp turnip called zoo-boo, the seeds of which the hanger-on around Panther Creek had once given us. Since we lived in the flat part of town, this was rich loamy Delta land, and our vegetables came out of it bountifully and fast. Daddy and I worked every late afternoon of the war until dark, chopping and weeding; Old Skip relished that garden, its fresh full aromas, following us down the rows as we worked, dipping his nose in the soil so that he looked like a dirt-dauber, sometimes going to sleep under the tomato vines or next to our scarecrow, with whom he had established a makeshift truce.

Every Saturday morning at ten o'clock there was the "Kiddie Matinee" at the Dixie Theater, and this, too, became a symbolic cosmos of the war effort. On the screen would be the latest chapter of the Spy Smasher serials involving grisly enemy agents, a newsreel of the fighting around the globe, and a full-length Western—Roy Rogers or Gene Autry or Lash LaRue or Don (Red) Barry. Many of the country people would bring their lunches in paper sacks and stay all day, right until sunset, watching Roy or Gene or Lash or Red all over again, joining the town children in cheering the inevitable scene in which the hero dashes across the range on his horse to rescue his friends from dismemberment or other catastrophe. If we collected enough coat hangers and tinfoil, which would be used to make bullets for our soldiers, and brought them to the Dixie Theater, the manager would let us into the Kiddie Matinee free of charge. Hence Skip and I would wander the alleyways of town twice a week or more, searching for discarded empty cigarette packages because of the tinfoil inside them; Camel cigarette packages were the most desirable of all because their tinfoil, it was said, made better bullets. I taught Skip to help locate these empty cigarette packages, and given his pervasive intelligence and diligence, which by now should be apparent to even the most jaundiced of readers, in little time at all he had mastered the search, bringing to me many empty packages in his teeth from the ditches, gullies, pastures, and undergrowth abutting our profligate alleys, as proud when he found one as the most princely young knight in quest of the Grail.

It was also integral to the Kiddie Matinee that if you agreed to perform in the talent show preceding the action on the screen, either you were permitted in without having to pay or, as was usually the case with my friends and me, who were already allowed in free because of our tinfoil, the manager would reward you with a dime, the price of the normal ticket. Often was the Saturday the others and I appeared in the talent show. This led to two salutary things: one, I could save my dimes and buy chocolate bars and bubblegum on the black market; and, two, the manager, finally convinced that Old Skip had himself contributed substantial quantities of the tinfoil, allowed him to come to the matinee with us. On four straight Saturdays Skip stood on the stage with Henjie, Big Boy, Muttonhead, and me as we sang a quartet rendition of "The Marines' Hymn," which we dedicated to all the marines in San Diego; "The Caisson Song" for the army in North Africa and England; "Anchors Aweigh" for the sailors in the Pacific; and "Off We Go into the Wild Blue Yonder" for all our pilots, navigators, bombardiers, tail gunners, and engine mechanics everywhere. Later, when the films came on, Skip would sit in the seat next to me, observing the transactions on the screen for a while before resting his face on my arm and going to sleep.

I often suspected that Skip had a natural compulsion toward repulsive smells, though not those as heightened as the skunk's, which had so debilitated him previously. The truth is, however, that he enjoyed wallowing in various peculiar substances and unusual elements and would come home with these vile odors on him—please do not ask me what. My mother refused to allow him in the house until these odors of their own accord wore off. It suggests something about the sweep of those war days, however, that my mother, who occasionally bought Evening in Paris perfume at the drugstore, would in such instances greet Skip at the door: "He's got Evening in Berlin on him again!" or: "Now, dread it, he's wearin' some Evening in Tokyo!"

As vivid as yesterday I remember the springtime Friday nights of school, my friends and Skip and I strolling along the broad boulevard in our blue-and-yellow Cub Scout caps on the way to a war movie downtown: *First Yank into Tokyo*, perhaps, or *The Fighting Seabees*, or *The Purple Heart*. The radios from the imposing houses blared the war news from London or the Pacific, or the words of Roosevelt or Churchill echoing out into the supple darkness, while Skip roamed among the wisteria or rhododendrons or tulips along the way. There was something in this I sensed, just a shred of boyhood emotion and memory: that in the echoes of the radios in the boulevard domiciles lay the fragile, beleaguered fate of us. How to know this then? It was there somehow in the trees and lawns, the birds and the wind chimes, the clouds and stars, and even in Old Skip's roamings in the dew-touched shadows. It was along this very boulevard, on another night, D-Day, 1944, that Henjie and Muttonhead and I tied tin cans to the end of a long string and pulled them along the middle of the street in a noisy commemorative parade, with Skip moving along right behind the cans.

The day the Japanese surrendered and the war was over, Skip and I were in the house with the old handyman, Tolbert, who was hanging some wallpaper. We waited all day for the announcement the radio said was coming. Tolbert was unable to get much work done because of the excitement, so we threw a baseball in the yard for a while, and shelled pecans, and shot a few baskets, and tossed sticks for Skip, and got him to climb the elm tree for squirrels, while the radio roared out at us from the bedroom window. Then Truman, the new president, came on and said the Japanese had given up, and Tolbert and I shouted and leapt and danced around and hugged each other, and Skip, catching the mood, leapt and danced around too. And we whacked each other on the back and leapt some more, and then I sent Skip to Bozo's for some bologna to celebrate.

······· 5 ·······

Chinaberry Fights, a Girl, and a Little Kitten

SKIP AND I were young then, and pretty much insepara-
ble, and took life on together, sometimes mindlessly, I
guess, as youth usually does, with all the absorbing reck-
lessness of being young. But we had quiet moments too,
mysterious and tender, and usually these were when we
were all tired out. Lying in the bed before sleep, hearing the
lambent whispers of the pecan trees in the breeze or the
haunting nocturnal call of the Memphis to New Orleans
train, I would put my hand on him and feel the beating of
his heart. He always loved to be rubbed on the back of his
neck, and when I did this he would yawn and stretch and
reach out to me with his paws, as if trying to embrace me.
What was he thinking about, I wondered. The day's adventures? The mischief-making next to come? My father had
built a tree house for us in our elm tree in back, a solid

plank floor nailed across two sturdy limbs, with a roof overhead of tin and fading branches. Often in the languid nights Skip and I would climb up to this private place and absorb the sounds of nature all around and look up at the moon. I would whisper to him about things of growing up.

One of those subjects was Rivers Applewhite. I had known her since we were two years old. We were in the fifth grade now, and she was the prettiest girl in our class, but she was not a demure kind of beauty. She wore her dark brown hair short, sometimes the way the models did in the library's copies of *Harper's Bazaar,* to offset her willowy grace. She had deep green eyes, and in spring and summer she was always brown as a berry from all the time she spent in the sun. She smelled of trees and clover and sunshine and grass. Since we had been around each other so long, I think she knew me almost as well as Skip did. I am also pleased to say she was not a tomboy; who in his proper senses would want a girl to kick a football farther than he could, or outrun him in the fifty-yard dash?

She was also very partial to Old Skip, and would bring him parched peanuts, and cotton candy when the county fair was on, and Skip was a regular fool about Rivers Applewhite, sidling up to her with his tail wagging, putting his wet black nose against the palm of her hand, jumping and gyrating in her presence like the craziest creature alive. Unlike some of the other girls, she would never so much as consider telling the teachers on anybody, and to this day I cannot recall a single traitorous or deceitful act on her part. Kind, beautiful, full of good fun and cheer, she was the best of feminine symbols to all the unregenerate boys. All of us, dogs and boys alike, were a little bit in love with Rivers Applewhite. I remember her in a white summer dress, one day shortly before Christmas, walking up a sidewalk of Main Street under the bright holiday tinsel. Skip and I were driving in our green DeSoto and saw her from half a block away, recognizing her from behind by the way she walked. As we got up close behind her near Kuhn's Nickel and Dime Store, I noticed that she *rippled* along that sidewalk, and that when she passed by people coming her way, just smiling calmly and being her jaunty self, they got a smile on their faces too. And when Skip saw her that day, he did something he never did before or since: he jumped out the passenger window of the car, landed impeccably on all four feet, and ran to her in affectionate salutation. So Skip knew Rivers, and the sound of her name, and when I whispered about her under the moon in the backyard, his eyes turned bright and he rummaged a little closer to me.

On his fourth birthday, she even gave a party for him in her backyard, inviting a dozen or so of the neighborhood dogs and their owners. The trees and shrubs were festooned with colorful balloons and ribbons, and from her kitchen she brought out a birthday cake consisting of separate layers of ground meat and bologna in the approximate shape of Skip himself, with four candles on top and the inscription

Happy Birthday, Old Skip! written meticulously in salted peanuts. We all sang "Happy Birthday" to him, and then Rivers put the cake on the ground for the honoree and the other dogs. That cake was gone in about forty-five seconds.

I have myriad other memories of Rivers and Skip together, and here are just two of them:

It was about six weeks after the end of the war, an early evening of halcyon October. It was a Friday and we did not have school the next day—a chilling evening with gusting winds, which made you feel good, and happy to be alive. We *should've* felt lucky to be alive, what with all the dead children and people all over the world, the starving neglected children wandering around sad, destroyed Europe that we had read and heard about, but I guess we did not know how really fortunate we were: I mean, just to have a chinaberry fight, and to be in America under a big moon with food enough to eat and friends all around, and a trusted dog like Skip, even if they *did* want to slay you with chinaberries. The harvest moon was perched like a huge orb at the horizon, orange and glimmering and bigger, it seemed, than the world itself. We had planned the chinaberry fight around my house on the boulevard, Rivers, Henjie, Bubba, Peewee, Big Boy, Skip, and the others. In a chinaberry fight you need a slingshot, with a tight long rubber band attached to the wooden Y-shaped base. Our next-door neighbor had the largest chinaberry tree in town. We picked the chinaberries from the tree and put them in a cardboard box before dividing them up. These chinaberries were hard and round as marbles, and when they hit you on the skin from a proper slingshot they really hurt. They stung almost as bad as a bee, and made puffy little blisters on the skin. In a chinaberry fight, when a berry from an opponent struck you, according to the rules and regulations of that long-ago day, you were dead, and presumably exempt from the fray.

Skip could do many things, but since he could not shoot a slingshot he was deemed a neutral in this combat, much, say, like the Swiss Red Cross. But this did not prevent him from his fervid relish of the developing scene, and he especially delighted in moving swiftly from one opponent to another in a vociferous dance, particularly when a direct shootout was imminent. With him as the sole noncombatant, we chose sides (I picked Rivers first), dug our individual supply of chinaberries from the box, and in the invigorating moonglow went our separate ways. In less than ten minutes I crept up on Henjie in the back alley and killed him with a chinaberry to the left nostril. He moaned and died. A few minutes later, as he lay cravenly shrouded in the tomato vines of our Victory garden, I dispatched Muttonhead with a shot to the abdomen. Then I began crawling on hands and knees toward my neighbor's house. Without warning Skip leapt out of the darkness onto my back and started barking. I pleaded with him to go away and not betray my whereabouts, and he forthwith did so. When I reached the house, I snuck into the thick shrubs at the side, lay silently on my back, and waited to ambush another adversary. I held my breath in anticipation.

I had been in my secret spot not very long when I looked up. I saw something that curdled my deepest blood. Just above me, only two or three feet away, was a gigantic spider-web. Even in the shrubbery it glistened in the ghostly moonlight. The web was thick and tangled, and in the middle of it was the biggest, meanest spider I ever saw. It was about the size of my clenched fist, with evil yellow stripes and tangerine coronets and a fiery green crown and menacing black dots on a pulsating body the color of that night's harvest moon. It was weaving back and forth in its great sinewy web. It seemed to be *writing* something in its own web! Was this the "writing spider" of the breed the old people had told us about since earliest childhood, which wove the name of its sorry victim before hypnotizing and then assaulting him with its deadly Delta poison? Even at that moment, the spider, with its skinny ebony legs and quivering green antennae and thousand surreptitious eyes, had seen me supine on the earth beneath it and was slowly descending toward me. Its venomous descent mesmerized me. I could not move or speak. I was paralyzed.

All around me I heard the shouts and yelps of my comrades being killed by chinaberries. I heard Skip barking in the distance, and prayed that he would come to me right now. I lay there breathless and suspended. The gigantic, hideous spider moved downward in its silken web. I lost all track of time. Long moments must have passed. A half hour? An hour? Both sides in the fight were surely long since dead; the game was over. I heard voices from far away: "Where's Willie?"

The spider was at the base of its web, examining me. I could smell its evil odor. My throat was choked with thick, cottony saliva, the saliva of abject fear. Then, from just outside the shrubs, I heard a friendly whisper, followed by another bark. It was Rivers—and Skip.

"He's around here somewhere," Rivers said. "Oh! There he is, Skip!" She later said she saw my feet protruding in the fallen leaves. "A writing spider!" she shrieked.

I felt her hands on my desperate ankles. She pulled me right out of there, just as the spider was about to leap onto my face. A long strand of web dangled from my nose, and I sneezed. Rivers laughed. "A close call!" she said. She bent down and hugged me. She had never done that before. "You even get in trouble with *spiders*."

But it was not over. As Rivers and I stood there, Skip thrust his nose into the shrubs and saw the spider. He began growling. *"Skip! No!"* Rivers and I shouted in unison. Before we could restrain him, he leapt wildly toward the spider. I was terrified, envisioning the characters S-K-I-P appearing any moment on the web. He tripped and fell, and now the spider began moving down toward *him*. Wordlessly I grabbed one back paw and Rivers the other, and we pulled him out of the bushes by his legs just as Rivers had pulled me.

. . .

One afternoon when Skip was three, a homeless starving kitten, three months old, perhaps, showed up at our back steps. Skip was lying in the shade of our elm tree when the poor little creature arrived. She was white and black like Skip, with translucent blue eyes, and she had been so neglected that her ribs were like ridges under her fur, and there was a raw jagged cut on her stomach. I was sitting on the steps and watched as the kitten walked right up to Skip.

I never saw such a transformation in him. Up till now he had been wholeheartedly indifferent to cats of all sizes and species, ignoring them to the point of regally walking away from them when they appeared fortuitously in our neighborhood, but when that little kitten hobbled up to him he rose and looked at her, then began licking her on the face, and when she lay down in the shade of the elm, he lay next to her. He felt sorry for her, I suppose, but he was also smitten by her, and his response to her struck something in me, too. The little kitten tugged at my heart.

Like Skip, I had had no experience with cats, and had been as apathetic to them as he ever was, but it took no genius with cats to see that this little one had just about given up. No one in my household knew about cats either—we were all dog people, and always had been—but Rivers had two cats, whom she doted on. I went inside and telephoned her, and she was there on her bicycle in five minutes. She examined the kitten, then held her closely in her arms. "Take care of her," she said. "I'll be back in a jiffy." She returned with an infant's milk bottle with a nipple on top, a can labeled "Milk for Motherless Kittens," and a tablespoon of medicinal ointment. In the next two or three days, I was touched by the sight of Rivers and Skip trying to nurse the diminutive visitor back to life. As Rivers fed her, Skip hovered about like an accomplished pediatric intern; that kitten could not have received better attention at the Mayo Clinic in Rochester, Minnesota. The kitten began to purr, and to move around with a little more spirit, and when she slept, it was in the crook of Skip's legs, not unlike the way he slept with me. Often the little kitten would gaze at Skip, and hug him with her paws. Rivers came every day for a week to check up on her. She named her Baby.

Suddenly one day, the kitten began to cough and retch, and then to tremble all over. As Skip gazed down at her lying on the grass, he nuzzled her with his nose, glancing up at me questioningly. Once more I telephoned Rivers. When she arrived, she held the kitten close to her. She died in Rivers's arms. Rivers started crying, the tears dropping down her cheeks in tiny rivulets, then put the kitten on the ground, and she, Skip, and I just stood there looking at her. I got a shovel from the Victory garden, and Rivers and I recited the Lord's Prayer before we buried her under the elm tree in the backyard. For weeks Skip acted sad and strange, and a very long while after that, in another city far away, Rivers Applewhite, whom I had not seen in twenty years, confessed to me she had never gotten over that kitten, and wondered if Old Skip ever had either.

When my mother eventually found out about Skip's and my confrontation with the writing spider, she banished all chinaberry fights in our neighborhood for two years. Even worse, along about then she took on eight more piano students, to the dismay of Old Skip and me.

My mother was of an old, aristocratic family that had been dispossessed after the Civil War. She was the best piano player in the state. Although we never suffered hardship, we were by no means rich, and she supplemented the family income by teaching piano. There was a Steinway baby grand in our parlor that occupied more than half the room. On late afternoons when it began to grow dark, Skip and I would listen to the music from up front. It was not the music the pupils repeated over and over that we heard, but the songs my mother played when she told the children, "Now *I'll* play your piece all the way through like Mr. Mozart would want it played." I can somehow hear her music now, after all the years, and remember the leaves falling on some smoky autumn afternoon with Skip there with me, the air crisp and the sounds of dogs barking and the train whistles far away.

It was the keyboard racket made by her students, however, that drove Skip and me to distraction. Rivers Applewhite was about the only one of them any good at the piano, and when she came to take her lessons, Skip and I would sit out of sight in the adjoining room and listen as she sweetly played her études and sonatas. The others were the most noisy and off-key creatures I have ever heard, and as they played their cacophonous exercises over and over, Skip's ears would twitch almost as agonizingly as they had during Hitler's radio monologues, and he would beg me to take him outside or anywhere else, for which I needed only scant excuse. One of the pupils, a tattletale in our school class named Edith Stillwater who had a small off-color wart on her nose, was playing so fiendishly one day that I thought the baby grand might go up in smoke; I cannot begin to describe those profane chords. Skip himself had had quite enough. His ears were making circular movements like miniature windmills. He rose from where he had been lounging on the carpet, slipped into the parlor, climbed onto the top of the piano, and in one of his famous leaps nose-dived onto the keyboard in front of which my mother and her tone-deaf protégée sat, accidentally making a chord with his paws and posterior that had more harmony to it than any ever contrived by Edith Stillwater. For this, supplementing the ban on chinaberry wars, he was made to sleep under the house at night for an entire week.

My mother also played the pipe organ in the First Methodist Church. Sometimes, early on Sunday mornings before anyone else arrived, Skip and I would walk down to the church and sit in a back pew in the empty sanctuary while she practiced under a beautiful stained-glass window. She played "Abide with Me," "Rock of Ages," "In the Garden." The music drifted through the tranquil chamber and made Skip and me drowsy, and we would stretch out on the bench and fall fast asleep.

In ecclesiastical circles, Skip was best remembered for a singular occurrence that elderly Methodists in the town, I am told, still to this day discuss. It happened during the regular eleven A.M. Sunday church service—in the summertime, before air-conditioning, a broiling forenoon of August, with all the church doors open. On the organ my mother was accompanying Mrs. Stella Birdsong, who had the most inappropriate surname in all the annals of music—a heavyset matron with an askew left eye, half-glass, half-real, it seemed to us, although that may not have been possible from the ophthalmological perspective—who was known in our area for her shrill, disharmonious high soprano notes, which caused chandeliers to rattle in her all-too-frequent performances. Henjie and I were seated on the aisle in a middle pew when he nudged me and pointed toward his ear as a signal for me to listen to something. Through the open door came the unmistakable sound from down the street of several dogs barking individually, and then in chorus, and getting closer by the minute. One of these barks, I perceived, belonged to Old Skip. Mrs. Birdsong had now begun her song, a sonorous religious composition with which I was vaguely familiar, which would be capped by a shrill, metallic high C at its apex. As she was approaching this culmination, suddenly Skip and five or six other dogs of our acquaintance, of all colors, shapes, and sizes, burst through the open door, all bunched together and sniffing at each other as they proceeded down the aisle. At that precise instant, as the dogs had progressed halfway down the aisle, Mrs. Stella Birdsong hit her lengthy high C, the most ear-splitting quaver I ever heard in my entire existence. And as she held on to it with the tenacity of an iron riveter, Skip and the other dogs stopped in their tracks, caught there in evanescent frieze, each of them turning his head in the direction of the singer. Then Skip, with a ferocity I had seldom acknowledged in him, lifted his snout and began to howl, and then the others joined in with him, howls of such devilish volume, and amplified by Mrs. Birdsong's continuing high C warble, that Henjie and I and others in the congregation put our hands to our ears. Just as swiftly as Skip and the other dogs had begun their wails, they turned about in concert and dashed out the door, and I could hear them still howling half a block away. From the pew behind us an elderly character not particularly known for his piety nudged my shoulder and said, "Them dogs got the old-time religion."

······· 6 ·······

Hazards, Dangers, and a
Very Close Call

THERE WERE OTHER hazards pertaining to Skip besides
Stella Birdsong and skunks, some of them of a more risky
nature. In the summer of his fifth year, for instance, he got
hit by a car, the only time that ever happened, the bumper of
it knocking him high in the air, and he somersaulted a
couple of times but landed squarely on his feet and walked
away chagrined but unscathed. Another time the Barbours'
big mean Doberman, who bore a striking resemblance to the
photographs I had seen of Hitler's dog Blondi, bit him on the
back of the neck and I had to take him to the same Dr. Jones
who had granted me Dog Care for a dozen stitches.

Once we were hunting in the woods when he suddenly
got mired in a small patch of quicksand. He frantically
clawed with his paws to escape, but the more he fought the
quicker he began to sink in that dark enveloping muck. It all
happened in a matter of moments. I did not have time to

panic, or even to tell myself to be clearheaded in the face of the appalling jeopardy to Old Skip—I believe I just *acted*. I tossed away my gun and shouted to my father to hold my feet while I lay down on my stomach in Skip's direction and caught him by the paw and gradually pulled him free. Only when it was over and he was on safe ground feverishly shaking himself to get rid of the grimy sand all over him did I sit down under a tree and take a deep breath, then and only then feeling the stark emotions of pity and terror.

There was also the frightening business of his encounter one day with a copperhead snake. He and I were driving around in the hills. In a certain area near Highway 49 there was one tall hill after another for many miles. All these hills and dark little valleys in between them were overgrown with a beautiful green creeping vine right up to the highway itself. This vine, known as the kudzu, sometimes grew onto the trees and telephone poles, making strange and wonderful shapes. Rumor had it that if a cow tarried too long in a field without moving around very much the vine would grow out so quickly as to cover the cow. The green creeping vine protected the land and kept it from washing away during heavy rains, but when I was a little boy I thought the whole town would someday be covered by it, that it would grow as fast as Jack's beanstalk, and that every person on earth would have to live forever knee-deep in its leaves.

Skip and I drove off the highway to a road right in the middle of that phantasmagoric green vine. I stopped in a clearing to let him run. Everyone knew that the vines were crawling with snakes, so I was not surprised to see a monstrous copperhead, one of the most poisonous of the indigenous species, slither out of the underbrush across the same clearing. I *was* surprised, however, to see Skip's reaction. Unlike what he did the day in the big woods when he sighted the rattlesnake and retreated a respectful distance to stare at it, he began to circle round and round this intruder, barking and growling. The snake did not like its privacy disturbed, and it snapped back at him, making ungodly hisses to match Skip's own commotion. He got closer and closer to the snake, ignoring my frantic shouts to get away. All of a sudden, in one prodigious leap, Skip came at the copperhead from the rear (just as, I had read in our library, Stonewall Jackson came at Hooker at Chancellorsville), caught it by the tail, and began dragging it all over the field. I could almost hear the fearful beating of my own heart, because every time the snake tried to bite back, his fangs extended in venomous rage, Skip would simply let go of it, and then move back in again to give the snake a couple of brisk additional shakes. While I was looking around for a rock to kill the copperhead, it headed out in a flash again, into the labyrinth of vines, wishing, no doubt, it had never left home. On the way back to town I gave Skip a stern lecture on snakes, but I knew it did not do much good.

I have mentioned that the town was half hills and half Delta. The name of the street that came swooping down out of the hills was Broadway, and it was the most unusual street of all. Its angle of descent was so steep that every so often the driver of some doomed car or truck would discover that his brakes were not nearly sufficient to deal with this reckless terrain. His path to death would be an agonizing one, as he whipped eighty or ninety miles an hour out of those hills, usually smashing into another car or truck where the ground leveled off at the intersection with Main Street. Once, as we were told it later as children, a truck full of cotton pickers got out of control coming down that perilous thoroughfare and crashed into a big pecan tree at seventy miles an hour; the dead and the dying were thrown for yards around, even into the broad leaves of the pecan tree.

Sometime during Skip's fourth year we were walking down the sidewalk of Main Street with Henjie and Peewee near this intersection when we heard a dreadful collision. We rushed to the site. A Coca-Cola truck had lost its brakes and smashed into the high concrete steps to the post office. The driver had miraculously escaped with minor cuts and bruises, which the Methodist preacher the next Sunday would describe as "a merciful act of the all-knowing Almighty," but the back door of the truck had been thrown open in the crash, and hundreds of Coca-Cola bottles were thrown out, most of them unbroken and rolling unencumbered along the middle of Main Street. At the sight of this grand bounty, Henjie and Peewee and I, Skip hot at our heels, raced into the Jitney Jungle nearby, where Big Boy worked sacking groceries, and got three of his largest sacks from him. Out in the street people of all ages and colors were picking up the unbroken bottles and running away with them. Skip watched as Henjie and Peewee and I, gathering and gleaning like squirrels, filled our sacks full of the Coca-Colas and carried them home. It was better than any Easter egg hunt.

A couple of years after that, Skip and I ourselves had our most formidable brush with disaster. I was driving the old DeSoto out of the hills toward Broadway; Skip was sitting on the passenger seat next to me. We were just beginning the descent when I casually pressed my foot on the brakes. Nothing happened. I pressed again, and again nothing. The brakes were not working! I pumped the pedal in terror as the car gradually began to gather speed; Skip put his paws on the dashboard and gazed quizzically ahead at the whole precipitous stretch of that street, and I began praying beseechingly to the Methodist Lord. Suddenly I remembered what my father had once told me to do in such an emergency. I switched off the ignition and slowly began to pull the emergency brake upward; the vehicle jolted once, then twice, throwing Skip against the dashboard. Had I not in that instant done something else, the reader would not have this book about Old Skip before him now, for this memoirist would not have endured to write it, nor for that matter would Skip himself have survived to be written *about*: I gently turned the steering wheel to the right and jumped the curb into Miss Sarah Cooper Lear's enormous side yard abutting the street, a treeless green expanse bereft of lawn furniture and even flowerbeds and bushes; I pulled up the emergency brake as high as it would go, and the DeSoto moaned and clanked and came to a reluctant halt halfway up a grassy incline. Skip and I just sat there for a moment, wilted wretches that we were, until Miss Lear came out and looked through the window and asked if we were all right. Neither I, Skip, nor the DeSoto had sustained a solitary scratch, and I sacked groceries at the Jitney Jungle all the next week to compensate Miss Lear for the tire ruts on her lawn, and attended church services the next eight Sundays in a row.

About the spookiest moment Skip and I ever lived through took place one appalling June night in the cemetery, scene of our previous pranks and hoaxes. Our cemetery, as I have earlier suggested, was one of the scariest in the South. Henjie, Peewee, and Muttonhead had gathered together all their financial capital and wagered me $8.50 that Skip and I would not spend an entire night in my army-surplus pup tent in the darkest and most fearsome section of the cemetery. I took that bet, because there were some items of furniture I wanted to buy for Skip's and my tree house, but only after my sadistic colleagues put me on the honor system, having me swear an oath on a Bible that I would not lie to them that Skip and I had fulfilled the obligation even if we had not, the reason for this chaste and upright declaration being, of course, that Henjie, Peewee, and Muttonhead were not about to visit the cemetery after dark to ascertain our veracity.

Part of the arrangement was that the three of them would accompany Skip and me just before the sun went down to select the most ominous spot. I carried with me the pup tent and a sack of provisions: a can of pork and beans, two Moonpies, some bologna for Skip, a can opener, and a canteen of water, plus two blankets and a pillow. To my dismay my antagonists gleefully chose the most forbidding place in the whole graveyard for me to pitch the tent: a gloomy glade not far from the witch's grave, with moldy nineteenth-century crypts and tombstones all around, and tall, ghostly trees, and dank, sinister shrubs and bushes. All this was part of one's worst nightmares. As I set up the tent in this somber and disturbing terrain Henjie said: "I'll tell you this, they ain't never gonna spend all night *here*. My share is two dollars and eighty-three cents." Then the three of them laughed, a chorus of righteous mirth. It was that unfortunate juncture between dusk and dark, close on to Midsummer Night, with still a little light at nine o'clock, and what was left of that light was fading fast, and formidable shadows were accumulating, and I was beginning to have second thoughts myself. I steeled myself to see it through. As the three of them turned to depart, Peewee chuckled and said, "Pleasant dreams!" As I watched them go, I noticed that only a few yards down the road they began to trot, and then to run because it was pitch-dark by now.

"Well, boy . . ." I said to Skip. I sat down by the tent and opened the pork and beans and gave Skip some of his bologna. A half-moon shone out over Brickyard Hill up

the way, casting over the whole graveyard a dread, shim-
mering aura. Lightning bugs were around us everywhere,
lending grotesque incandescence to the surroundings.
Not far away a mockingbird began her nocturnal song. I
had always loved mockingbirds, and so had Skip, sitting
under our elm tree in the backyard in the summer dusks,
absorbing her sweet, adoring call. Who would ever want to
kill a mockingbird? But on this encompassing night in the
graveyard her lovely voice suffused me with trepidation, as
if she were only *mocking* Skip and me in our vigil at the
pup tent.

Skip seemed to be having the time of his life, and this
angered me: he strolled audaciously among the tombstones
and even jumped on top of the gray, lugubrious Darrington
crypt to survey the scene. The least anxious thing to do, I
concluded, was to climb into the tent and force myself to go
to sleep. As I lay down on the blanket I was aware of danc-
ing shadows and the swirling rustle of leaves. Shortly Skip
climbed into the tent and snuggled next to me, and I was
glad to have him there, I can tell you.

I must have fallen into a long but fitful slumber, filled
with odd, shapeless wisps of nightmares, suffused with the
sound of shovels digging into earth, when I was suddenly
awakened by Skip's rising from my side, and as I anxiously
peered through the darkness I saw him standing at the
entrance to the tent silently looking out, taut and pointing
the way he did with the squirrels in the big woods. I glanced
at my Woolworth's wristwatch; it said quarter to two. I

crawled toward him and looked out too. What I saw in that moment in that cemetery chilled me in the blood as nothing in my whole life ever would.

About fifty yards away I made out the form of a battered pickup truck parked at the side of the road. Then, off to the left of it, I sighted four strange men in work clothes bending down before something. In that instant a cloud drifted away from the moon. I tried to rub the heavy sleep from my eyes. Were they actually digging up a grave?

In my impenetrable fright I tried to ponder what to do. Skip was still standing next to me. I recalled the words in a movie I had once seen at the Dixie about the United States Military Academy at West Point: *Duty. Honor. Country.* I remembered, too, my Boy Scout oath as it related to conscience and obligation: "On my honor I will do my best to do my duty to God and my country." These words resonated now in my brain. Perhaps I could identify these insufferable grave robbers. "Let's get closer," I whispered to Skip. "Don't make a noise."

Stealthily the two of us crawled in the direction of the villains. We were only twenty-five yards or so from them and hiding behind a tombstone: *Robert Stacy Yarbrough, 1831–1899.* From the farthest distance down in town I could hear the courthouse clock chiming two A.M. I glanced out again over the top of the tombstone. The silhouettes of the four figures were clear to me now. One of them had a gruesome pockmarked face, another a red mustache, but I had never once seen any of them, and from the place-name on the license plate of their pickup truck, they were from a county many miles away.

Then, to my horror, Skip began to bark. He growled, then barked some more. I tried to put my hand around his mouth, but in the act of doing so I stumbled and fell out from behind the tombstone, then looked desperately up and realized that the men had seen us. The one with the pock-marked face began walking swiftly in our direction. In seconds he was standing over me.

"Well, look at this!" he said. "Come join the party!" He gazed down the way. "You been sleepin' in a *pup* tent? This is some crazy town." He dragged me by the hand and staggered toward the pickup truck. His three companions amiably greeted me there. They were drunk as could be. My deceived eyes in the cemetery's gloom had convinced me they were robbing a grave, but what they were really doing was drinking beer out of long bottles and getting drunker all the while; I dared not ask them why they had chosen a graveyard in the middle of the night for these revels, and on quick reflection acknowledged I myself would find it difficult to explain my own presence, not to mention my dog's, in these circumstances. One of the men was feeding Skip some peanuts and potato chips and making him feel at home; and then he handed me an opened bottle of beer and told me to take a swig, which I obediently did, and then another. It tasted awful. After the deranged hallucinations of that night, one thing I did not need was beer.

It also must have put me into a long and leaden sleep. I awakened at the first glimmer of light to the sound of roosters up on Brickyard Hill. Somehow my back was propped against a tombstone, and Skip was sound asleep with his head on my lap. I glanced around. The pickup truck was gone and there were empty beer bottles all over the place, and a quart jug with a little corn whiskey left in it.

I will tell you what else was gone too: my pup tent, blankets, pillow, water canteen, can opener, moonpies, and the rest of my pork and beans and Skip's bologna. Henjie, Peewee, and Muttonhead dutifully gave me the $8.50, but with all my losses that night I calculated I was down by three dollars at the least, and it eventually took me two years to finally confess to them about the grave robbers.

In this recitation of perils and misadventures and hallucinations, I have postponed the most disturbing until last because even with the passage of the years I find it difficult to write about.

About nine o'clock one evening I went out in the backyard to find Skip lying limp under our elm tree. He looked awful. Perhaps he had grown tired in our interminable journeyings around town, and he also must have consumed something bad, some stricken water somewhere, some rotten food maybe. His nose was dry as dust, and so were his paws. I lay on the grass with him and felt his stomach. It was hot and feverish. Also, little strands of warm saliva were dripping down his mouth, bubbling as they flowed. "Wait, boy." I went inside and brought back a bottle of aspirin and a wet towel. He was shaking all over now. I put two aspirin under his tongue and made him swallow them, then applied the wet towel to his face.

My father had been working late at his office, and when he arrived home he came outside and looked him over. "I think he's got hold of some poison," he said. He telephoned Dr. Jones, but he was attending a veterinarians' convention in Memphis. Then he called the all-night animal clinic in Jackson and described the symptoms. They said to rush him there right away.

My father got in the driver's seat of the DeSoto; I sat in the back and held Skip in my lap. Jackson was forty miles away, much of it over the same steep hills with the creeping vine where Skip had attacked the copperhead snake. The vines were sere and gray now in the winter's cold, and the night hushed and desolate under ponderous clouds, and we raced through the bare little villages as fast as we dared. "Don't die, Skip," I said, and he looked up at me with glazed eyes. After an eternity, it seemed to me, we reached the outskirts of Jackson; far in the distance was the state capitol, brightly lit and imposing, like a picture postcard against the frigid sky. When we arrived at the animal clinic we took him inside. A young veterinarian asked us to wait and took him in back. He returned several minutes later.

"It's poison, all right."

"Who would want to poison a dog?" my father asked.

"Only bad folks," the doctor replied.

"Can you cure him?" I asked.

The doctor said he was not sure. Skip was very sick. He would give him the best medicines he had. If he survived the night he would live. He advised us to drive on home and come back the next afternoon. My father and I made the journey home in a grim silence. Alone in my room I missed Skip asleep in the crook of my legs. As on the day the brakes had given out on the DeSoto, I prayed to the Lord. I promised Him I would behave myself forever if He would save Skip. I hardly slept that night, and the next morning I did not go to school. That afternoon we drove again to Jackson. At the clinic I held my breath as the doctor greeted us.

"I've never seen a dog come back like that from poison," he said. "That dog wants to live." He needed to be nursed a few days, he said, and he gave us two big bottles of pills. All during the following week I made him rest on the sheets in my bed. I brought him water and bologna cut into small pieces and a bedpan to relieve himself, and Rivers and the boys brought him wildflowers. Then, bright and early one morning, I felt him licking my nose as he always did to wake me up. When I opened my eyes he was sitting there next to me wagging his tail. The impish expression in his eyes had returned, and he bit my toes to roust me out faster. "Let's go chase some *squirrels,* Skip!" I said, and he leapt off the bed and waited for me to take him outside—from the valley of the shadow of death he had returned to me once more.

Old Skip and Baseball

HE WAS A DOG for all sports seasons. Ralph, the photographer in our group, once captured this quintessence in him, having him pose under the oak in my front yard with a St. Louis Cardinals baseball cap on his head, the lace of our football grasped between his teeth, his paw in a baseball glove, and in front of him on the grass a basketball, a baseball bat, four baseballs, my baseball spikes, a tennis racket, a volleyball, a football helmet, half a dozen or so sports magazines and game programs, and numerous baseball bubblegum cards.

I had even created a mythical dog football team of my own devising, consisting of various dogs I was familiar with in the town, and often when walking somewhere alone or riding on my bicycle I would entertain myself by reciting play-by-play accounts of games involving this team, which I called Kennel U. Using my mother's old Kodak camera, I went around taking snapshots of the dogs on the team, pasting them into the crude replica of an official game program, with thumbnail sketches of each dog, such as Sheriff Raines's Buck and the Hendrixes' Super-Doop. We operated out of the single-wing offense made famous by the Tennessee Volunteers. Skip was the tailback and, naturally, also the captain.

His dramatic touchdowns in our real football games in my front yard were fabled in the town, of course, but he also enjoyed watching the boys and me shooting baskets around the wooden basketball goal in back, and whenever someone made an errant shot that missed the entire backboard and bounced over the hedges toward the front, he would enthusiastically retrieve it and push it back to us with his nose. His swiftness and agility were likewise legend, and when of the spirit he could move so fast that I desired some specific authentication of his actual speed.

I borrowed Henjie's father's stopwatch one Saturday morning and persuaded some of the fellows to accompany us to the high school football field, where I intended to time Skip formally in the hundred-yard dash. The difficulty was that I knew I must improvise some method that would get him to race from one goal line to the other, exactly one hundred yards, at top velocity and in as straight a path as possible. How to do this? At first I had Henjie, Big Boy, and Peewee station themselves at the far goal line with the stopwatch while I positioned Skip at *our* goal line, in as close an approximation of the classic sprinter's stance before the starting gun as I could persuade him to assume. Then, on a signal from me, our three companions began shouting, *"Skip, come here!"* at which I would give him a vigorous shove to get him on the way. This did not prove efficacious, producing a series of false starts in which he might sprint fifteen yards in the right direction, or twenty, or twenty-five, then circle around and return to me. After a reflective conference the others and I arrived at the proper solution. Pee-wee would hold Skip at the starting line, with Big Boy and Henjie at the opposite line with the stopwatch. I would station myself at midfield and shout for Skip to follow me, then start running toward Big Boy and Henjie, and at that precise moment Peewee would release Skip, who would likely run after me in a straight line and at full acceleration for the entire distance.

This indeed worked perfectly the very first time we tried it. I yelled at him from the fifty-yard line and then began running in the opposite direction. The instant Peewee released him Henjie started the stopwatch. I ran as fast as I could, but in little time at all I could hear him approaching me from behind. I crossed the finish a mere three or four strides before he did. Then, with Peewee dashing alone down the field toward us in his keen curiosity, Big Boy and I approached Henjie, who had the stopwatch extended in his hand and was grinning with such wild felicity that I thought he might commence jumping up and down at any moment.

We looked at the stopwatch: *7.8 seconds!* Take into consideration if you will that the *human* world record in the hundred at that point in history was 9.4 seconds, held by a fellow named Mel Patton. I immediately surmised that the all-time world record for fox terriers was achieved on that day in this small-town high school football stadium of the American Southland. Who would have the audacity to question it? We did, after all, have four witnesses.

You will have to take me at my word, however, that his favorite among all the sports was baseball. How did I know this? Because I knew my dog very well, and it had to do with the look in his eye when he was around baseball, and also with that particular time and place.

Like Mark Twain and his comrades growing up a century before in another village on the other side of the Mississippi, my friends and I had but one sustaining ambition in the 1940s. Theirs in Hannibal was to be steamboat men; ours in our place was to be major-league baseball players. In the summers, we thought and talked of little else. We memorized batting averages, fielding averages, slugging averages; we knew the roster of the Cardinals and the Red Sox better than their own managers must have known them; and to hear the broadcasts from all the big-city ballparks with their memorable names—the Polo Grounds, Wrigley Field, Fenway Park, Yankee Stadium—was to set our imagination churning for the glory and riches those faraway places would one day bring us. Soon after the war was over Peewee went to St. Louis on his vacation to see the Cards, and when he returned with the autographs of Stan Musial, Red Schoendienst, Country Slaughter, Marty Marion, Joe Garagiola, and a dozen others, we could hardly keep down our envy. I hated Peewee for a month and secretly wished him dead, not only because he took on new airs but because I wanted those scraps of paper with their magic characters.

I had bought a baseball cap in Jackson, a real one from the Brooklyn Dodgers, and a Jackie Robinson Louisville Slugger, and one day when I could not locate any of the others for catch or for baseball talk, I sat on a curb with the most dreadful feelings of being caught forever by time—trapped there always in my scrawny and helpless condition. *I'm ready, I'm ready,* I kept thinking to myself, but that remote future when I would wear a cap like that and be a hero for a grandstand full of people seemed so far away I knew it would never come. I must have been the most dejected-looking boy you ever saw, sitting hunched up on the curb and dreaming of glory in the mythical cities of the North. And Skip, of course, would be right there on the street curb with me, dreaming his own dreams. Sometimes he would sit in my lap when I listened on the radio at home to the Cardinal games out of KMOX in St. Louis. When the boys and I played catch in my front yard, he would sit on the porch, watching us with interest, and often as not he would go inside and bring back his tennis ball and have us toss him his own grounders and high flies. Ever since he was two years old he could catch a tennis ball in his mouth as well as any center fielder. I had started him off on this gradually. He was about a year old when I began throwing the ball on a bounce from short distances, then moving a little farther back every day. At first he muffed most of them, but soon he became all but unerring. After that I started gently tossing the ball to him in the air. Then we progressed to short pop flies, and finally to tall, arching throws way up beyond the topmost branch of the oak tree, which Skip dexterously circled under, his eyes following the lengthy descent, snaring the ball when it reached him, then dropping it in front of me before I again threw it to the tallest heavens for another acrobatic catch.

Almost every afternoon when the heat was not unbearable my father and I would go out to the old baseball field behind the armory to hit flies. I would stand far out in center field, and he would station himself with a fungo bat at home plate, hitting me one high fly or Texas Leaguer or line drive after another, sometimes for an hour or more without stopping. Old Skip would get out there in the outfield with me and retrieve the inconsequential dribblers or the ones that went too far. Once my father hit one so long that it bounced on the pavement of the street beyond the outfield and rolled three blocks away, and I watched as Skip had to run a quarter of a mile at least to retrieve it, eventually bringing it back to me and dropping it at my feet.

The smell of that new-cut grass was the finest of all smells, and Skip and I could run forever and never get tired. It was a dreamy, suspended state, those late afternoons, thinking of nothing but outfield flies as the world drifted lazily by on Jackson Avenue. Then, after all that exertion, Daddy would shout, "I'm *whupped,* and the dog is whupped, too!" and we would quit for the day.

On Sunday afternoons my father, Skip, and I sometimes drove out of town and along the hot dusty roads to baseball fields that were little more than parched red clearings, the outfield sloping out of the woods and ending in some gully full of yellowed paper, old socks, empty bottles, and bugs. One of the backwoods teams had a fastball pitcher named Eckert who did not have any teeth, and a fifty-year-old left-handed catcher named Smith. Since there were no catcher's mitts for left-handers, Smith had to wear a mitt on his throwing hand. He would catch the ball and toss it lightly into the air and then whip off his mitt and catch the ball again in his bare left hand before throwing it back.

In his gregariousness Skip developed a fondness for the toothless pitcher and the southpaw catcher, often coming down out of the forlorn unpainted little bleachers to watch them warm up before a game, and to sit between them on the bench when their team was at bat, where they shared with him their parched peanuts. It was a fine way to spend those Sabbath afternoons—my father and Skip and I sitting behind the chicken-wire backstop with a few farmers and their families, watching the wrong-handed catcher go through his odd gyrations and listening at the same time to our portable radio, which brought us the day's action from Yankee Stadium or Sportsman's Park. The sounds of the two games, ours and the ones being broadcast from far away, merged and rolled across the bumpy outfield and the gully into the woods. It was a combination that seemed perfectly natural to everyone there.

Because back home, even among the adults, baseball was all-meaning; it was the link with the outside. A place known around town simply as The Store, down near the train depot, was the principal center of this ferment. The Store had sawdust on the floor and long shreds of flypaper hanging from the ceiling. Its most familiar staples were Rexall supplies, oysters on the half shell, legal beer, and illegal whiskey, the latter served up, Mississippi bootlegger–style, by the bottle from a hidden shelf, and costing not merely the price of the whiskey but the investment in gas required to go to Louisiana to fetch it. There was a long counter in the back. On one side of it, the white workingmen congregated after hours every afternoon to compare the day's scores and talk batting averages, and on the other side, also talking baseball, were the blacks, juxtaposed in a face-to-face arrangement with the whites. The scores were chalked up on a blackboard hanging on a red-and-purple wall, and the conversations were carried on in fast, galloping shouts from one end of the room to the other.

An intelligent white boy of twelve was even permitted, in that atmosphere of heady freedom before anyone knew the name of Mr. Justice Warren or had heard much of the United States Supreme Court, a quasi-public position favoring the Dodgers, who had Jackie Robinson, Roy Campanella, and Don Newcombe—not to mention, so it was rumored, God knows how many Chinese and mulattoes being groomed in the minor leagues.

We often went there to get the scores and absorb the animated repartee, and this unlikely establishment was one of Old Skip's favorite spots in town, ranking right up there with the dump, the fire station, Bozo's grocery, and the Victory garden and tree house in our backyard. Intrigued by its variegated activities, he would accept the raucous affections of the town drunks and petty gamblers as if they belonged to him alone, but when one of them offered him some raw oysters one day, he took a couple of sniffs, made a face, and imperiously went outside to wait for me.

As I got older and into high school, I was the center fielder for our team. Our coach was nicknamed Gentleman Joe. He always had us pray before a game, and sometimes between innings when the going got rough. His pep talks, back behind the shabby old grandstand of our playing field, drew on such pent-up emotions, being so full of Scripture and things of the holy earth, that I sometimes suspected we were being enlisted not to play baseball but to fight in the Army of the Lord.

Given this spiritual emphasis, Skip acutely distressed me on this very baseball field one afternoon, in a historic scene more rampant by any measure than the morning he and the other dogs came down the church aisle during Mrs. Stella Birdsong's ill-fated soprano solo. We were playing host to the juggernaut team from the metropolis, Jackson, and there must have been four or five hundred people in attendance, including the big-city partisans, who condescendingly viewed us as small-town unsophisticates. We were about halfway into the game, and leading it by a score of 1–0, when the progress of it was precipitately disrupted.

The Jackson boys were at bat and I was at my post in center field when out of the corner of my eye I saw Skip himself burst out from under the left-field bleachers and run madly in my direction. The playing field was at least two miles from our house, and how he even knew about the game I will never comprehend, except for his almost psychic propensity, previously cited, for fathoming where in the various venues of town I might approximately be at any particular moment. As he raced onto the field, the base umpire called time and began running angrily after him. Skip came right up to me to offer his salutations. I tried to chase him away. *"Go home!"* I shouted, and when the umpire finally accosted him, he started circling the outfield in widening arcs, then rushed to the infield to pay his respects to Muttonhead at shortstop.

Muttonhead tried to catch him too, but Skip eluded his grasp and ran up to Big Boy on the pitcher's mound. By now the whole playing field was in pandemonium, the other umpires joining the chase, and Peewee from second base, and Henjie threw off his catcher's mask and went after him, and Gentleman Joe, and Sheriff Raines, and even Rivers Applewhite, who later said she thought she alone could tame the miscreant, and after a while numerous of the enemy players took to the pursuit, losing their caps as they did so. Only my friends and I on that field appreciated how elusive Skip could be when he chose to, but they persisted in the hunt. Four or five of this posse would momentarily surround him, but he would squirm through their legs, or dash away with his world-record speed, while in the grandstand the spectators cheered and applauded, and the waggish public-address announcer put on the music "Take Me Out to the Ballgame." I was so chagrined I cowardly watched the spectacle from deepest center field, not once moving to assist, until he galloped out in my direction once more, and stood there just looking at me. I was exasperated. I reached down and smacked him on his rear, the first and last time I ever did so, and as he glanced at me, as if I were the rankest of turncoats, I grabbed him firmly in my arms, whispering *"Go home!"* all the while, and ran to the nearby outfield fence and tossed him over it. Then, standing on my utmost tiptoes, I peered across the top of the fence as he walked slowly through the cotton field beyond, halted once and looked back at me with a betrayed and wounded countenance, and haughtily began ambling in the direction of home. We subsequently lost that game 10–1, and for long days my friends and I held Old Skip accountable, Big Boy complaining that after the tumultuous interruption he misplaced both his curveball and his control, but since we lost most of the other games too, Skip was after a decent time forgiven.

.... 8 ....

Christmases

WE LOVED THE TOWN at Christmas, in the clear, cool air, the lights aglitter in front of the established houses on the hills and down in the flat places, the sudden containment and luster. Skip would accompany our church group as we went caroling, and as we observed the heavenly path of the star, it must have been *the* star, as it moved across the skies from around Belzoni out in the Delta, up over Brickyard Hill and Peak Tenereffe; sung on such a night, the Christmas carols were the most peaceful blessings in all the world. Our friends and I and Skip would take Christmas baskets to poor people living in shabby little cabins in the hills and feel glad that our families were not in such bad straits. Rivers Applewhite, Skip, and I had a custom on Christmas Eve of walking down Main Street to look at the bustling crowds and the decorations, then out into the residential sections to see the Christmas trees in the windows. The town seemed expectant, all laid out and still under the pristine December night.

A few days before one Christmas it snowed: this was for us a most rare and majestic event. I had seen snow once before, when I was very small, but most of the younger children never had, and they went wild with joy. Skip had never seen snow either, and I observed him as he pranced in it on our lawn, rolled about in it, and tried to catch the flakes in his mouth. I went a little berserk myself and started shooting baskets in the backyard in it, enjoying the sound of a successful shot made through the frozen basketball net. The next day Skip and I trudged to the top of Brickyard Hill with a sled. He sat in front of me and I held him tightly as we descended in an exuberant swoop all the way down to the cemetery. We did it again and again, returning home exhausted from the countless treks to the apex of the hill. That snow, if you can believe it, lasted on the ground for four days, and the older townspeople still remember it with reverence.

Christmas mornings were warm with the familiar ritual. We would wake up shortly after dawn in our house—my father, my mother, Skip, and I. Skip would have aroused me out of sleep with his nose as always, then bitten my toes, then pulled the blankets off me with his teeth to make sure I would not tarry any longer. No worry about that on *this* day. We would open the presents, and Skip would have his own stocking: a new tennis ball in it, perhaps, and a package of bologna and fried chicken livers, and a new collar. My mother would play three or four carols on the baby grand; then we would have the sparsest of breakfasts to save room for the feast to come.

Under the purple clouds we would drive the forty miles south to Jackson to be with my grandmother Mamie, my grandfather Percy, and my incorrigible great-aunts Maggie and Susie. The drive itself is etched in memory, the same we took the night Skip was ill—the tossing hills and the frost on the ground and the tiny hamlets on the plain with their wan, lost facades where children played outside with their acquisitions of the day, and finally the splendid glimpse of the Capitol dome and the ride down State Street to the little brick house on North Jefferson. When Skip saw the familiar house he would bound out the car door swift as a fox, and I was not far behind.

They would be there on the gallery under the magnolia tree waiting for us, the four of them, and we would all go inside to exultant embracings to exchange our gifts, modest items for sure, and examine what we had given one another. Once Skip got a rubber mouse that squeaked, and proceeded to bite it in two. And the smells from the kitchen! The fat turkey and giblet gravy and cornbread stuffing and sweet potatoes with melted marshmallows and the orange nectar and ambrosia and roasted pecans and mincemeat pies! Skip hovered around the oven while nibbling on a roasted pecan and my two great-aunts, who could not see very well, bumped into each other every now and again and wished each other Merry Christmas, while the rest of us sank into the chairs by the fire in the parlor and awaited what my grandmother was making for us. Christmas songs wafted from the chimes of the church down the way, and the crackle of firecrackers came from the neighboring lawns, and my grandmother would dart out of the kitchen with Skip at her heels and say, "Almost done now!"

Then, at eleven in the morning, never later, we would sit at the ancient table, which had been my great-great-grandmother's: my grandfather Percy and my father at opposite ends, my mother and great-aunts on one side of it, my grandmother and I on the other, Old Skip poised next to my chair, expecting his favors. Occasionally I would slip him a turkey gizzard or liver or wing. We sat there for two hours, it seemed, prattling about many things. The clock on the mantel would sound every quarter-hour, and my great-aunts would ask for more servings and say, "My, ain't this *good?*" I would look around every year at each of them, and feel Skip's nose on my hand, and listen to the talk, as if all this was designed for the two of us alone. Then, after the rattling of dishes, and after Skip had dined on leftover dressing and pieces of turkey, we would settle in the parlor again, drowsy and fulfilled, Skip stretching out on the carpet in his Yuletide torpor. Finally my grandmother, standing before us by the fire, would gaze about the room and always say, in her tone at once tender and bemused: "Oh, well, another Christmas come and gone."

The Changing Seasons

"TIME, HE IS A TRICKY FELLOW," Lewis Carroll said. Old Skip had come to us when I was nine years old; by the time I entered high school, I was fourteen and he was four. If, as the authorities often declare, a dog's life in relation to a human being's can be calculated by seven human years to his one, then Skip was twenty-eight when I was fourteen. This is all too confusing, however, and I intend not to place much stock in it: my memories of Skip move in and out and around in time anyway, from my grade school years through junior high and high school and beyond, which is likely as it should be, because if the existence of all creatures is a continuum, there is still plenty of room to weave and backtrack and drift and glide. Life is indeed a confluence, but seldom a steady one, and embraces forever the changing seasons.

. . .

Autumn: Our region of America never had the great flamboyant, bursting beauty of northern autumns, but there was a languor to our Octobers and Novembers, especially in the dry falls when the foliage was so profound and varied, and the very landscape itself would be imbued with a golden, poignant sheen.

One Saturday during the autumn I woke up quite early to take full advantage of the fresh, free Saturday ambiance, and in such a disposition *I* woke up *Skip* rather than the reverse, and we lounged around in bed for a few more minutes as I considered the day's unique possibilities. My room was quite small but nonetheless contained an unusual number of interesting items: colorful pennants from a dozen colleges; the German helmet and belt hanging from nails on the wall; horns from a dead cow; a photograph of the 1946 St. Louis Cardinals; my father's old baseball glove; a bookcase with books by Mark Twain, Zane Grey, Dickens, and Poe; the rattlers from the rattlesnake I had killed in the woods; four chunks of petrified mud picked up along ancient creekbeds; and various photographs of Skip with Rivers Applewhite, the other boys, the bulldog Buck with whom he had shared the first prize in the dog contest, and myself.

Lying there in bed with Skip beside me, I gingerly recalled the major events of the day before. After school Friday he had been waiting for me at his appointed place on the boulevard. We immediately went home and got my bicycle and rushed out to the black high school football field to see the Black Panthers play a game and to imbibe the lavish flair of their players and fans. They played in the discarded uniforms of our high school, so that their school colors were the same as ours, and they even played the same towns up in the Delta that our high school did. Skip and I normally sat on the sidelines next to the cheering section, but one afternoon the referee asked me to carry one of the first-down markers, and Skip followed closely beside me during that entire game as I fulfilled these official responsibilities. Next I conjured the scenes from last night's white high school game, which Skip, Peewee, and I had watched from the end-zone bleachers, and the infectious undercurrent of excitement there, for on Fridays in the fall you could almost feel this tension in the atmosphere, the unreserved reverence for the game itself, the awesome thuds of big old boys running headlong into each other, the off-key marching bands, the cheerleaders making pyramids of flesh, while all through this pandemonium the spectators slapped at the manifold Delta bugs attracted from the nearby swamp-bottoms by the lights of the stadium.

At about nine o'clock I got dressed in a pair of blue jeans, tennis shoes, a white T-shirt, and a green baseball cap with a Y on it. Skip and I ate some raisin bran in the kitchen; then I led him outside for a lengthy session of retrieving sticks. It was Indian summer and everything—the earth and the trees, touched by the airy sunshine—was the lazy golden-brown of that sad and lovely time; there was the faint presence of smoke everywhere, and the smell of leaves burning, and sounds and their echoes carried a long, long way. Wherever you looked there was a truckload of raw cotton coming in for ginning; along the country roads and even the paved avenues in town you could see the white cotton bolls that had fallen to the ground. The county fair was on, and every night that week we had taken in the 4-H exhibits—the vegetables, and the bottled preserves of all the shades of the rainbow, and the pumpkins, and the great slabs of meat. How Skip loved those county fairs! He strolled the grounds with the other boys and me in a spirit of fine titillation, ate the cotton candy Rivers Applewhite gave him, and waited impatiently while we took the carnival rides. I had tried to get the man who ran the Ferris wheel to let him go on it with us, but he was not sympathetic. "This contraption ain't no place for a dog."

In our backyard on this Saturday morning Skip was by now a little tired out from his exertions, and it was time to consult with Henjie. I went into the house and told the telephone operator his number (it was 27; mine was 243; my father's office was 1). When Henjie answered the phone, I wanted to know if everyone was coming to the football field, and he said they would all be there at ten; we had stopped going to the Saturday Kiddie Matinee when the war ended and we felt we had outgrown it anyway. I fiddled around with the radio awhile, and read the *Memphis Commercial Appeal* for the football scores; then I got on my bicycle and headed up the street toward the football stadium, with Skip following, stopping every so often for him to examine a dead frog or some other lifeless object or to greet an old lady.

When he and I reached the field, the same site at which he had earlier set the world record for fox terriers, we ran a few wind sprints, then examined the cleat marks that had been made in the turf the night before by our high school heroes. Three thousand people had been in these grandstands and the bleachers just a few hours ago! I did a pantomime of a forty-three-yard scoring play, dodging Skip and the imagined tacklers on last night's exact route to glory. Then the boys showed up, including Peewee with his official Southeastern Conference football with the dangling lace for Skip to carry in his mouth on his running plays, and we chose up sides and played a brisk brand of tackle until the twelve o'clock whistle blew at the sawmill. The only injuries on this day were to Peewee's big toe, which he claimed he sprained when tripping on a cleat mark, and to Henjie's head, which he said Big Boy had mistaken for the football. The final score was 86–69, my team over Muttonhead's.

The afternoon held many possibilities, but this one began with fried chicken and biscuits and other delicacies at Bubba's house, for his mother's refrigerator contained a plethora of riches mournfully absent from the one at my

WILLIE MORRIS

house, and then an interlude listening to the Ole Miss or State football game on the radio, because there has always been a religiosity to college football in our region, and Saturday is the holy day. After that we rode our bicycles to Main Street to see the latest Boston Blackie movie, then returned to my house to get our DeSoto and take a spin around town, from the telegraph shack at the end of Main Street to the Country Club at the rim of the Delta. Only a scant minority of its citizens had never seen Skip behind the steering wheel, but we managed to locate a little store on Brickyard Hill which was virgin territory, and the inevitable old man shouted: *"Look at that ol' dog drivin' a car!"* Then we proceeded to Henjie's house to listen to the college football results on the radio. We lounged on his front porch and watched the leaves drift from the oak trees and listened indolently to the scores—first those of the little schools in the East like Williams and Colby and Amherst and Niagara, or Allegheny and Susquehanna and King's Point and Lafayette; then the Ivy League scores, which were just exercises; on to the big midwestern and southern ones that really mattered—moving slowly across the country like a great roll call of America.

After that Skip and I took off for home, walking down the hills toward the quiet flat streets, and making it just in time for hamburgers and french fries. After supper I turned on the lamp in the front yard and put the portable radio on the porch, tuning it to the LSU game from Tiger Stadium

90

in Baton Rouge, and Skip and I played football again by ourselves, I making up the whole game to the accompanying din of the thousands from the radio, racing ninety-five yards for fictitious touchdowns before seventy-five thousand cheering fanatics, intercepting enemy passes in the dying seconds of the fourth quarter, kicking forty-six-yard field goals against thirty-mile-an-hour winds. By now it had been a long autumn Saturday. Old Skip and I stretched out on the cool, wet grass. I used the football for a pillow and he lay down beside me and we gazed up at the stars until it was time to go in to bed.

In remembering moments such as these, I retain the sad-sweet reflection of being an only child and having a loyal and loving dog, for in the struggles of life, of the dangers, toils, and snares of my childhood hymns, loyalty and love are the best things of all, and the most lasting, and that is what Old Skip taught me that I carry with me now.

And the coming of the springtime for Skip and me in that old town! Even today it is an echo in my heart: the prolific chorus of the land, which sang like a living being; the overpowering fragrances of the vines, flowers, and grasses; the early jonquils and flowering quinces and then the blossoming pears and dogwoods and azaleas; the incessant cadence of the katydids in the nights; the broad lawns glistening with dew; the lightning bugs in late spring flickering and vanishing as far as the eye could see.

Skip and the fellows and I took long rambling hikes up to Peak Tenereffe on the old valley road, which once had been an Indian trail, and stood high on the bluffs and looked out over the dark fecund Delta land being broken now for the cotton planting, and absorbed the rich odors everywhere of the honeysuckle and wisteria, coming back down only when the lights of town one by one twinkled on far below. Or we walked up the bayou, which had been dug deep into the earth to bring the waters down from Brickyard Hill past the cemetery, through the residential section, past the cotton gin, and on to the river. In these springtimes, with the water coming out of the hills, the bayou was crawling with hundreds of crawdads, and Skip sometimes went after them, circling around them as he had with the copperhead, until one afternoon one of their number pinched his nose with a claw, and that was it for him and crawdads. We walked under one bridge after another, following the source of the water until the bayou itself ran out. Then we played by ourselves or with the other boys in the empty cavernous cotton gin by the Illinois Central tracks, or strolled down Highway 49 to inspect the floodwaters from the river, the overflowing gullies and the shacks with stilts as uneasy protection against the cascading waters. On Thursday evenings in the spring Skip accompanied me to the Boy Scouts meetings in the church, and afterwards participated with us in the loud and strenuous games of capture the flag and kick the can on the school grounds, once taking the empty can in his mouth and running away with it, so that we had to go to a neigh-boring house and ask for another can.

In the springtime there was nothing gentle about nature. It came at you violently, or in a rush. When the muddy waters from the river invaded the town, and even the shacks on stilts in the bottoms were covered over, we saw the open trucks with the convicts crowded in the back on their way to bolster the levees with sandbags, their black-and-white stripes somber under the gray, forbidding sky. Sometimes a tornado twisted down and did strange things to whatever it hit, carrying someone fifty yards and leaving him barely hurt, or driving straws into car tires like needles, or sending our garage across the alley into a field of weeds.

One afternoon a modest tornado descended while we were watching a movie in the Dixie. We heard hailstones on the roof, hitting in steady torrents. All the lights inside turned dim, and after a succession of emphatic thumps the movie on the screen broke down. We got out of there, onto the sidewalk under the front marquee. Skip, who had been waiting for us, as was his custom, was standing there bark-ing. In the middle of Main Street bicycles were floating in midair up and down the whole thoroughfare, and Skip, like the spectators at tennis matches who turn their heads right and left while following the ball, was bobbing *his* head back and forth as the bicycles whizzed past. Then the wind began to subside, and a huge rat, caught in the waters of the gutter, was being carried by the strong current closer and closer to the sewer that would transport him into the river. Skip went out and watched as the rat disappeared, and on the walk home, with trees strewn everywhere, he pushed at the egg-sized hailstones with his nose.

Skip managed to get in everywhere. In school I was away from him for long hours, and he did not like it at all. A disastrous incident happened to me one April when I was in the fifth grade. We had a considerably mean-spirited teacher named Miss Abbott. One day when she was out of the classroom I made a spitball and threw it two rows over at Edith Stillwater. At that precise instant the wretched Miss Abbott came back into the room and shouted my name; the sound of her voice sent terror to my soul.

Each afternoon for six weeks during that incomparable spring I had to "stay in" for two hours, working long division. Miss Abbott would sit at her desk, reading the Bible or *Reader's Digest,* while the shadows got longer and the sound of the boys' voices at play wafted in through the open windows. On one of these afternoons, who should suddenly burst into the classroom but Skip himself, angry, I suppose, that I had been getting home so late in recent days; he approached me at my desk and licked my hand; then he spotted Miss Abbott and started growling contemptuously at her, prompting her to throw down her *Reader's Digest* and retreat into a corner. In a querulous voice she ordered us both to leave, and the next morning she added another whole week to my incarceration.

A few years after that, during my first year in high school, our English teacher, Mrs. Parker, asked our class to stay after school an entire hour for a special spelling bee. It was a glorious late afternoon of mid-May, and we were not even halfway finished when Skip leapt through one of the open ground-floor windows and landed on his feet near Rivers Applewhite's desk, knocking off all her schoolbooks before walking to me. Happily this teacher, unlike the brutish Miss Abbott, was a kindly personage and lover of dogs, and she said: "Welcome, Skip! Can you spell?" The intrusion was a fortunate one for me, because just before his histrionic entrance I had been called upon to spell *purification*. Skip's interruption gave me time to decide that there was only one *r*, rather than two, in *purification*.

As Summers Die

FOR A BOY AND HIS DOG—need it even be said?—the summertimes were the best of all. They came and went for Skip and me in splendid random, touching our mutual boyhood and our getting older with the patina of the passing days.

Three or four times every summer he and I went to Jackson to stay with my grandparents and great-aunts. We always took the Greyhound bus to Jackson. Being a friend of my father's, the driver allowed Skip to make the journey on the bus—the price was a quarter for me and a dime for him—and the loudspeaker in the station just before we boarded would always say: "Central Local Bus now loading on Platform One—for Little Yazoo, Bentonia, Flora, Pocahontas, and *Jackson*-town!" and off we would go.

Though quintessentially a small-town dog, as the reader by now may have discerned, Old Skip was adequately sophisticated for the capital city, thank you, and reveled in its own distinctive summer adventures. Our Christmases there had already suggested to him, I can't help thinking, that if grandparents are noteworthy for spoiling a grandson, they can be equally solicitous of the grandson's dog. My grandmother catered to his every whim and foible, which included giving him canned shrimp, potted meat, and even collard greens on occasion, so that by the conclusion of our summer sojourns he had assumed a spirit so magnified and grand that I knew I would have to get him back to more earthly reality on our return home.

To me, my grandfather Percy was old, older than almost anyone I had ever known, but he never let on that Skip's and my pace was more than he had bargained for. He would do everything I wanted, from climbing the fig trees in the backyard to marching down the street beating a dime-store drum. He worked in the place on Griffith Street that made potato chips. Every afternoon at four he would come home smelling of potatoes, and would fetch from his old leather satchel two big bags of chips for Skip and me, crisp and hot. Sometimes he would take the two of us to work with him, and we would watch while he put on his white apron, carry the great sacks of peeled potatoes to a machine that cut them into thin slices, and then transfer them to the prodigious black oven that heated up the finished product. We munched on potato chips all day, from nine to four, and came home so full of salt and potato grease that we had to drink half a gallon of ice water at supper.

Maggie and Susie, my grandmother's eccentric old-maid sisters, were challenges, I could tell, to Skip, and he always observed them quizzically in their ceaseless and directionless peregrinations. They had been born long ago during the Civil War, and neither of them could hear or see very well, getting me confused with a brother of theirs who died in 1908 and Skip with a dog named Beauregard they had owned as girls in 1879; once they even confused Skip with a *cousin* of theirs who had passed on during World War I. They perambulated inside the house and around the yard all day long in their fantastic flowing dresses, running into doors and trees, knocking things off tables; sometimes they bumped into each other in these interminable explorations, and said "Excuse me," and then pushed off again in opposite directions. Several times a day they tripped over Skip, and once when I saw Maggie trying to strike up a conversation with the garbage can in the backyard, Skip was sitting there moving his head back and forth, and when he saw me he seemed to be asking, "What's going on here?"

We took long walks, my grandparents and great-aunts and Skip and I, down streets shaded by crepe myrtles, where old ladies on decaying verandas would sometimes ask us in for iced tea; and on to the State Capitol with its fine air of permanence, to search for envelopes with foreign stamps on them in the big refuse bin; and on to the cemetery down the way in the hot, glowing dusks; and then the long walks home, Skip leading the procession because the varied topography of the big town had long since been amply planted in his brain.

If the years of World War II, in Skip's and my childhood, were glorious beyond measure in our own town, they were equally stimulating in the capital city. Jackson was crowded with soldiers of all ranks and origins, and one could hear the clipped Yankee accents all along East Capitol Street, and on several occasions my grandfather and Skip and I walked out to the German prisoner-of-war camp to gaze at the captured soldiers behind the high fences; on one of these afternoons a sergeant of the Afrika Korps bent down and tried to pet Skip through the barbed wire, insisting in his halting English that he reminded him of his own dog in Germany.

In addition to the northern accents that filled the down-town, you heard the Dutch tongue all around you, because hundreds of pilots from Holland were training at the air base, and exiled Dutch leaders were living here also. One morning my grandmother took Skip and me to the Jitney Jungle across the street, which she used for all practical purposes as her personal pantry, visiting it several times a day to buy a tomato, or a head of lettuce, or a cucumber, but mainly to gossip with the other ladies of the neighborhood, and at the vegetable counter with two other perfectly dressed women, she pointed out to me, was the Queen of the Netherlands! I told Skip this, but I doubt that it regis-tered, and if it did, that he believed it.

At night, as Percy and Skip and I lay half-awake in our beds, I could hear their voices—Mamie's and my great-aunts'—from the parlor. My great-aunts' world was unexpectedly clearer at this hour, and I loved to lie in the next room, in that lulled awareness just before sleep, and hear the tick-tock of the old clock and the quiet, eclectic talk: about Momma and Poppa, or the other brothers and sisters long dead, or the one brother who went to New York at the turn of the century and was never heard from again, or the family house in Raymond, sold those many years ago. Percy would groan in his half-sleep, and recite "Oh, to be a child again just for tonight." It was like shifting gears, from boyhood's concerns and the war with the Germans to a different world filled with Yankees, poverty, and death. Later, if I woke up in the middle of the night, I heard snores of such a variety and intensity as were never heard before—tenor and contralto from the back room where Mag and Sue slept, playing to Percy's staccato bass—and moans and sleeptalking into the early hours, and Skip would nuzzle close to me as we listened some more. I knew that Skip and I would never grow old.

And then back home again on the Greyhound.

I can still see the town now on some hot, still weekday afternoon of midsummer: ten thousand souls and nothing doing. Even the red water-truck was a diversion, coming up the boulevard with its sprinklers on full force, the water making sizzling steam-clouds on the pavement while half-naked little children followed the truck up the street and played in the torrent till they got soaking wet, Skip sometimes joining them in this mindless charade. Over on Broadway, where the old men sat drowsily in straw-bottomed chairs, whittling to make the time pass, you could laze around on the sidewalks—barefoot, if your feet were tough enough to stand the scorching concrete—watching the big cars with out-of-state plates whip by, the drivers hardly knowing and certainly not caring what place this was. Way up that fantastic hill where Skip and I had once lost the brakes, Broadway seemed to end in a seething mist—tiny heat mirages that shimmered off the asphalt. On Main Street itself only a handful of cars were parked here and there, and the merchants and the lawyers sat in the shade under their broad awnings, talking slowly, aimlessly, in the cryptic summer way. The one o'clock whistle at the sawmill would send out its loud bellow, reverberating up the street to the bend in the river, hardly making a ripple in the heavy somnolence.

Summer for us was considerably more solitary than the fall, since so many people were out of town on vacation—but what was wrong with that? By nine o'clock we were out of bed and on the move. First I made Kool-Aid in a large glass pitcher, gathered some old comic books, and put my mother's folding card table under the tree in the front yard. On the table I taped a sign that said: *Funny books, 3 cents, Kool-Aid, 2 cents a glass*. While Skip, so hot that his tongue dripped with sweat, drowsed under the table, I might get three or four sales by noon, but rarely did commerce thrive in that stifling heat. In the early wartime years, to pass the time between sales I killed flies with a flyswatter, pretending that the flies were Japanese fighter planes, bagging twenty-three in ten minutes one morning near a watermelon rind, or turned over a flat stone and killed ants with a hammer, pretending they were German footsoldiers trying to establish a beachhead. After a while the two of us just sat in the shade of the tree and watched the morning pass by: the red water-truck, horse-drawn wagons heading to town, a group of dogs all bunched together going to the dump. Skip, if of the mood, would socialize with them for a little while. Soon we heard the ice-cream man coming around the corner with the bell on his cart ringing, and if I had cleared a nickel's profit on our morning's sales I would purchase a Fudgsicle and share it with Skip. At noon it was time for a glass of Kool-Aid and a ham sandwich, and some chicken livers for him, and then to amble into town to see what was going on, with me walking along the sidewalks and superstitiously avoiding all the cracks, and finally taking a shortcut down the bayou to Main Street.

One day we were standing on Broadway and Main when I spotted a quarter at the bottom of a sewer. I went to the alley behind the Dixie and found a long stick, stuck the wad of gum I was chewing on the end, and returned to the sewer, where, after considerable maneuvering, and with Skip hunched down and gazing at this operation with his usual curiosity,

I speared the quarter with the gum and with a vigorous yank brought it out. With these unexpected earnings I hailed the ice-cream man again, who by now had made it all the way across town from our house, and this time bought *two* Fudgsicles, one for me, one for Skip. Then, for a nickel, because the driver let Skip ride free, we boarded the new city bus on Jefferson Street and rode in much excitement and pride, since the town had never had a bus line before, up Main and Canal and Brickyard Hill and the boulevard and down Canal to Main again: the limits of our world.

Now we went to my father's office, where I experimented for a while with his typewriter; then on to the radio station to read the news coming in from all the world's capitals on the teletype and to hear the announcers promote the virtues of various insecticides and fertilizers and a spectacular locally made patent medicine that cured everything from gallstones to summer itch; then to the offices of the newspaper to observe that week's issue coming off the flatbed press; and next to the ice house, where on especially scalding days the boy who worked there allowed us to spend a few minutes in the room where they made ice, a dark, frigid, timeless chamber a universe removed from the blazing summer world outside. There was a cotton auction taking place at the auction center, the first of the year, and we watched that for a few minutes: the staccato warble of the auctioneer, the men in khakis milling around in clusters, discussing the quality of that summer's product. Then to the Armenian's to watch him make bread, and to the Italian's to watch him make coffee, and to Gregory's Funeral Home to watch a funeral procession get started, and to the courthouse to watch part of a trial from an empty balcony, and to the Catholic church to look into the windows and get scared. Once Father Hunter himself caught us at one of the windows and gave us a tour inside: the unfamiliar statuary, the alien baptistery, the faint incense odor. Then to a big open field right in the middle of town to play among the rows of cotton bales waiting to be hauled up to Memphis on the train. Then on to the Ricks Memorial Library, where the ancient ladies permitted Skip to go to sleep under the long oaken table in the reading room while I read the latest serials in *Open Road for Boys*. Then up to the firehouse to visit the firemen, playing dominoes while listening to a ballgame, who in their gregarious indomitability had put aside their embarrassment over the fact that the firehouse itself had partially burned because of faulty electrical wiring the previous summer, and who more often than not gave me a Nehi Strawberry and Skip a nibble of ham or hard-boiled egg. Finally, on the way home, we might stop at Bubba's, who would by now be back from weighing cotton at his father's plantation, and we might bake some more oatmeal cookies using our standard recipe of castor oil, milk of magnesia, and Skip's dog-worming medicine, then gift wrap them and put them on some mean old man's front porch.

On the Fourth of July there was always a political rally in some large and dusty clearing in the middle of the woods.

The barbecue and potato salad and sliced homegrown tomatoes and corn on the cob and biscuits were stacked on long tables and served up by country people, and I sat on the grass with this steaming feast in my lap, splitting some of it with Skip, lethargically eating and listening to the preachers and politicians.

But mostly we liked the little creeks and streams that trickled out of the hills into the flatland, and most of all the river itself in the summertimes, the river of the vanished Indians, the Yazoo, which flowed slow as could be past the giant cypresses and elms and weeping willows, southward toward the Mississippi. We basked in the sun along these banks and watched the boats drift by. Why did the gnarled, bending cypresses always seem to be trying to tell something to me? It was a river not to be tampered with, but it had a grace to it nonetheless: the way it opened up and wound around, the moss hanging over it from the cypress trees, the decaying old houses along it that Skip and I explored. One of these houses stood only a few yards from the river, with a ruined sagging veranda and high ceilings and an oak tree that had grown tall through a collapsed place in the roof and these words carved on a wall in what must have been the kitchen: *Your cause is a hard one and I pity you. Lt. Thompson. Illinois 36th Inf.* We were in this house one day when a heavy thunderstorm came, and the trees all around and even the old house itself swayed and moaned and the river beyond made rippling murmurs.

One summer after I had reached high school I served as "public relations director" for the town's recreation park, where I was chief assistant to the high school football coach, and supervisor of a radio program each afternoon. The park was only three or four blocks from our house, and Skip and I strolled over there every morning that summer. He became a fixture among the children as he observed with interest their softball games and Ping-Pong matches and shuffleboard and horseshoe throws; some of them called him Uncle Skip. The football coach and I, accompanied by Skip, collected a carload of children every day at four and went to the radio station for our daily broadcast. We interviewed them about their participation in that day's various activities and announced the winners and their scores.

The program was a hardship, however, on those days when no children at all turned up at the park; then the football coach and I would have to talk to each other on the air for half an hour, about anything we could think of that would fill up that time. During these broadcasts Skip sat on the floor under the microphone. After a long silence one day when we were depleted of things to discuss, the coach asked, "Skip, what did you do at the park today? *Skip!*" and with that loud declarative Skip began to bark at some length, and the disgruntled radio station manager was later heard to comment, "Now they're interviewing *dogs*." Once the coach and I talked for five minutes about a Ping-Pong table we had just nailed back together, and then about a bark blight a certain elm tree near the shuffleboard had caught, and another time we discussed at some length why the Nicholas children, who lived just across the street from the park, failed to show up on that day. The football coach surmised that they had probably gone out of town for a while; no, I speculated, I had seen them that morning eating Popsicles in front of a grocery store. On one particular day when it had rained for several hours and no children whatsoever came to the park, the football coach and I, with Skip in the backseat, cruised all over town in his car looking for a child to interview. We had run out of talk ourselves, and anybody would do.

Ten minutes before our program was to go on the air, we spotted a little boy walking up Main Street in the rain. It was Donnie Fulton, who spoke with a stutter. The coach drove the car up to the curb and shouted, "Donnie, come get in with us." The little boy dutifully got in the car, and the coach whispered to me, "Don't let him go now we've got him." The boy made a motion that might have suggested escape, but Skip, sensing something a little untoward perhaps, growled the boy into tentative submission. We trundled him down to the station and interviewed him for twenty minutes.

One night that same summer Skip and I were sitting on the front porch when suddenly we saw a large Delta Airlines passenger plane as it began curiously circling low over our neighborhood, then started an odd descent toward our dirt airstrip two miles away. What on earth was this meant to be? I ran to the DeSoto in the driveway, Skip following closely behind, and we sped out to the airport just as the passenger plane came to a skidding halt in the muddy runway. Everyone, like us, who had heard its motors had also reached the airport as the lost plane landed—we later learned the pilots had mistaken the lights of town for the Jackson airport forty miles south. A sizeable crowd had gathered near the airliner. Henjie's father, who was president of the chamber of commerce, was carrying a stepladder, and when Skip recognized him he followed him toward the plane. Henjie's father put up the ladder and said to each frightened passenger as he climbed down it into the mud, "Welcome to our little town." The next week there was a photograph in the newspaper, on the top of page one, of Henjie's father and Skip greeting the passengers.

During one of these summers before the tenth grade Skip accompanied me to Camp Kickapoo, the Boy Scout camp situated in deep sequestered piney woods thirty miles south of us, for our annual organized outing. The scoutmasters knew him from our weekly meetings and our brisk intervals of kick-the-can afterward and said it would be fine to bring him along. He really admired that scout camp—the nightly sessions around a roaring fire when the scoutmasters told ghost stories and recited "Casey at the Bat" and "The Barefoot Boy," the raucous play, the swimming pond where the others and I practiced our strokes for the coveted merit badges. I had been appointed the camp bugler responsible for reveille and taps, and Skip faithfully climbed the hill with me before every dawn when I sounded my notes on my silver trumpet to rouse the slumbering boys, and again at night to induce them into reluctant sleep. On the evening before we left for home, as we sat around the fire, the members of the troop unanimously voted Skip an honorary Boy Scout. There was a heartless price to be paid, however, when we got back into town, for Camp Kickapoo richly deserved the nickname it had been given through the decades: Tickapoo. My father discovered about two dozen ticks on Skip's back and stomach, several of them severely bloated, and even found several on *me,* one behind the lobe of my ear. "Ticks are a bad business and deserve to be respected," he said, and forthwith drove us down to Dr. Jones, the vet, who one by one removed them from us by modern hygienic methods.

The intrepid Henjie and I had taken canoeing lessons from the scoutmasters at Tickapoo, and just before the start of school that year we borrowed his older brother's canoe for an excursion down our river. We would spend the night camping out. We accumulated our provisions, including the usual sliced bologna for Skip, and put into the river just below Main Street. Skip sat between us, as well-behaved as he had ever been—*reflective*, almost, it seemed, much as he had been that day long ago on the steps of the deserted tenant shack after the storm—as we slowly paddled out from town into the encompassing countryside. This was another of those memories that would last, a memory of the spirit, really, and not so much of the brain; I guess it had to do with the very earth itself. Amid the surrounding swamplands and thickets the grassy banks of the bayous were lined with the familiar willows, and the duckwood was thick and emerald green in the melancholy brakes of cypress, and the cattails danced in the whispery breeze. Turtles lay in the sun on logs in the water, and when two or three of them concluded to get up and jump in the river, Skip observed them with his quizzical lift of the face.

It was early September, and there was the most subtle touch of autumn all round. You could not see it in the leaves, but you could sense it: a vagrant coolness, evanescent light and shadow. Henjie and I pretended that I was Tom, Skip was Huck, and he was Jim, even though he was not the proper color. In the distance were old Indian mounds where we had come as children in search of arrowheads and earthen fragments of pottery; in the eternal flatness they resembled miniature grassy hills. On both sides of us in the great fields the cotton blossoms were beginning to turn white. Dozens of black people were chopping with their hoes, and Skip's ears twitched as their muffled song drifted out to us:

> I ain't got too long now, I ain't got too long . . .
> I ain't got too long now, I ain't got too long . . .
> The man be comin' for me soon.

Farther on down, in the dwindling afternoon, Skip dipped his snout into the brownish muddy river for a drink of water, then unceremoniously spit it out: "too thick to drink, too thin to plow," I had read in Mrs. Parker's class on what Mr. Twain said of the bigger river to the west, so I poured some water from one of our canteens into a container for him. With the arriving darkness we tied the canoe to a cypress and camped near some willows, and after supper Skip drowsily settled in the crook of my legs and we went to sleep to the sound of Henjie's snores and a million cicadas.

One evening of high summer when I was in the eleventh grade Skip did not come home. I had not seen him since morning. In all our years together this had never happened. I asked my father if he had seen him.

"He's probably off chasing squirrels," he said. "He'll be back."

I telephoned Rivers, Henjie, Peewee, Muttonhead, Bubba, and Big Boy, but he was not with them. After supper I went out looking for him on my bicycle. I rode all over town, calling and whistling for him everywhere. I could hear my own sad echo off the facades of the accustomed old houses and buildings: *Skip, where are you?*

I rode everywhere that he usually went when he made his rounds. There was a boxer puppy on Main Street that he liked to visit. And a Scottish terrier on Calhoun Avenue. And a big, shaggy dog, part Lab, part Saint Bernard, that he admired on Jefferson Street. And a hybrid old hound on Brickyard Hill. All over town people were outside watering their lawns, and I asked if they had seen him. I half-expected to see him coming out of someone's yard, bounding through the bushes when he heard me whistling. But he did not come. I rode until dark before I gave up. I put my bike in the garage and sat on the front steps until bedtime waiting for him. I telephoned Sheriff Raines, telling him of my missing dog. It felt strange to go to sleep without him in bed with me. I was used to pushing him out of the way so I could turn over. That night the bed seemed too big for me. I tossed and turned all night, sitting up every time I heard a noise, hoping it was him scratching at the door to be let in. I remembered the night he had been poisoned, and the time we had saved him from the quicksand in the woods.

At first light the next morning I began riding around again, retracing my earlier routes, then going on to the football field and the cemetery and the bayou and the dump and the waterhole and the river and the park and every alley in town. I made more telephone calls. I went to the backyard and sat under the elm tree, alert for any sound of him. Had he been run over on some country road? Drowned in the river? Bitten by a copperhead? *Kidnapped?*

I had to give it another try. Once again I got on the bicycle and began riding in a neighborhood of dingy shacks not far from the dump. I had already been there the day before, but I repeated the search, calling out for him all the while.

In a desolate stretch of this vicinity something suddenly caught the corner of my eye: an old, rusty, abandoned refrigerator at the edge of a vacant field. I had noticed this derelict refrigerator three or four times in our recent journeyings around the locality, but the sagging door to it, I recalled, had always been ajar. I was drawn toward it compulsively now, as to a magnet. I got off the bicycle and approached it. I was not sure, but I thought I heard something inside, some strange rustling movement—or was it my imagination? I could hear the pounding of my own desperate heart. I reached out and yanked open the door.

Who should leap out of that refrigerator but Old Skip! He was a little limp and weak, and when he saw it was me he crawled slowly toward me and lay at my feet. I got on my knees and rubbed him around the lungs, the way we had been instructed in first aid in the Scouts. He gulped in the fresh air and began wagging his tail. He was all right! We remained there a long time, until the whistle from the sawmill across town blew. I shivered at the thought of what had happened. In his normal investigative spirit he must have crawled into the refrigerator, his movements causing the door to close behind him. He had been trapped all the time in that awful refrigerator—he could have been dead in a few hours. What must he have been thinking in his insidious entrapment? Was he just waiting there for me to come?

"Skip," I said to him, "please never leave me again!"

······· 11 ·······

Going Away

WHY, IN CHILDHOOD and youth, do we wish time to pass quickly? We want to grow up—and yet again we do not. This is the way people are, and have always been, even before the telephone, television, electricity, jet airplanes, and fax machines. You want to grow older, and yet you don't. Can anyone explain it?

As my high school years began to close, Skip remained constant in his companionship. Rivers Applewhite and I, too, were a steady pair. When we double-dated with Big Boy and Daisye, or Muttonhead and Janie Sue, riding around town on Saturday nights along the streets of our childhood, Skip rode around with us, until we let him off at my house and went on to the midnight movie at the Dixie. Our baseball team won the state championship that year, and in the parade down Main Street, with the crepe paper decorating the lampposts and the marching band playing our fight song, he rode in the back of a flatbed truck with my teammates and me. They gave the team shiny red-and-white jackets with *State Champs, 1952* on the back, and he loved that jacket so much that when I spread it out for him on the floor or the bed he would go to sleep on it, and on chilly nights I would wrap it around him with only the top of his head above it. At the graduation ceremonies in the school gymnasium that June, when my friends and I marched down the aisle in our mortarboards and gowns to the strains of *Tannhäuser,* he tried to go inside but was mindlessly turned away. Afterwards, however, he attended the midnight-to-dawn dance, a tradition at graduation among all the boys and girls in all the Delta towns of that day, with its black jazz bands and matronly chaperones and exhilarating air of ceremony and frolic, and Skip stayed up all night with the rest of us.

I went to college in another state far away. For our first paper in English composition the professor assigned us a two-thousand-word autobiography; I began with a description of the fading lonely sunlight outside my dormitory window, went back through the years with Skip, and concluded with much rhetoric in the same dormitory six hours later. One sentence read: "My dog and I wandered the woods and swamplands of our home shooting squirrels." To which the teacher appended the comment: "Who was the better shot, you or the dog?" When I telephoned my parents from college, they got Skip to bark at me from the other end. When I came home in the summers we did the same old things, but it was different—not that I was not as close to him as I had been, but that I was not a boy anymore, and that the whole outside world was beckoning to me.

And that Skip himself had somehow grown old. He was eleven when I graduated from college, and feeble, with arthritis in his legs. Sometimes he still had the devilish look of eye, but he did not retrieve sticks anymore, and preferred lying in the shade of the trees, or under the steps to the back door, and he did not want to ride in the car, and he never woke me up in the mornings; it was I who had to wake *him* up.

> In a wonderland they lie,
> Dreaming as the days go by
> Dreaming as the summers die.
>
> Ever drifting down the stream—
> Lingering in the golden gleam—
> Life, what is it but a dream?

I won a scholarship to England to complete my studies; I would be away three years. The day came when my parents had to drive me to meet the train East, where I would take an oceanliner. I knew I would never see Skip again.

My parents were waiting in front of the house when I went to the backyard to say good-bye to him. He was lying under our elm tree, the one in which he had trapped Bubba and me years before, with the same old tree house up there, a little forlorn and neglected now. I sat beside him not far from the grave of the little kitten we had buried those years ago and rubbed the back of his neck, in the spot he had always wanted to be rubbed. He lifted his head and looked at me, then put his head in my lap, nuzzling me with his nose as he had done the first time I had seen him as a puppy. I told him I had to go and that I would miss him. He looked at me again, and licked my cheek. "Thank you, boy," I whispered. Then I left without looking back.

But as the car pulled away from the house, I looked back. Skip was walking along the front lawn, and then sat down and gazed at me. I watched him until he was just a tiny speck.

A month later there was a transatlantic call for me at Oxford University. I went to the front lodge of my college to take it. "Skip died," Daddy said. He and my mother had wrapped him in my baseball jacket and put him in the ground, close to the grave of the little kitten.

I wandered alone among the landmarks of the gray medieval town. A dozen chimes were ringing among the ancient spires and cupolas and quadrangles, all this so far in miles and in spirit from the small place he and I had once dwelled. Walking alone in the teasing rain, I remembered our days together on this earth. The dog of your boyhood teaches you a great deal about friendship, and love, and death: Old Skip was my brother.

They had buried him under our elm tree, they said—yet this was not totally true. For he really lay buried in my heart.